OKINAWA

Flashpoints

The end of the Cold War unleashed a new era of international relations and accelerated the forces of globalization. Old conflicts reasserted themselves and the seeds of new threats were sown. This series examines those regions, relationships and issues that in the international arena have the potential to cause conflict between states. Each title offers a theoretically grounded analysis of the history, current complexion and likely outcome of the flashpoint to enrich our understanding of global politics, security and international relations.

Published

The Kurds: The Struggle for National Identity and Statehood
Mandana Hendessi

North Korea: Survival of a Political Dynasty
Ramon Pacheco Pardo

Okinawa: Great Power Competition and the Keystone of the Pacific
Ra Mason

Syria: Realism in Action
Neil Quilliam

Taiwan: A Contested Democracy Under Threat
Jonathan Sullivan and Lev Nachman

OKINAWA

Great Power Competition and the Keystone of the Pacific

Ra Mason

agenda
publishing

For Nakki

First published in 2025 by Agenda Publishing

Agenda Publishing Limited
PO Box 185
Newcastle upon Tyne
NE20 2DH
www.agendapub.com

ISBN 978-1-78821-784-2 (hardcover)
ISBN 978-1-78821-785-9 (paperback)

British Library Cataloguing-in-Publication Data
A catalogue record for this book is available from the British Library

Typeset by JS Typesetting Ltd, Porthcawl, Mid Glamorgan
Printed and bound in the UK by CPI Group (UK) Ltd, Croydon, CR0 4YY

Contents

Preface

This book is the culmination of my ongoing research and experiences living on, travelling around and interacting intensively with Okinawa since 2001 when I first visited the islands from Tokyo as a young person in the midst of a hot and hectic Japanese summer. Ever since that time, the role and meaning of this unique island and its extended archipelago – positioned at the very centre of a geological and geopolitical fault line that runs through the stunningly serene beauty of the East China Sea's turquoise iridescence – has fascinated and enthralled me. Now, as the geopolitics of the Far East threaten to boil over from a new cold war to hotly contested kinetic conflict, it seems appropriate to focus attention more than ever on what is poised to become one of the region's key flashpoints.

The concept for the book was, therefore, to create an informative, engaging and balanced resource for those new to Okinawa who want to learn more about it and its heightened significance. However, I also anticipate that practitioners, academics and students who might want to better understand the complexity of Okinawa's state, market and societal spheres will find the text to be a useful resource, as well as containing a compelling argument, namely that Okinawa matters! Through this project, I have aimed to challenge existing literature on Okinawa that suffers from specific or partisan perspectives and compile a single volume that is both holistic in nature and integrated in its approach. In addition to those at the head of government, directors of large corporations and military leaders, it is my belief that only by incorporating the role of a wide range of key actors from foreign policy-making, domestic political and business communities, as well as the broader general population, can realistic counter-measures and sustainable solutions be developed in response to escalation. Only then can the currently tense status quo be alleviated and a lasting peace be realized.

In order to successfully realize this challenging endeavour and express it in a credible form, the research unpacked throughout the chapters that follow consciously and systematically accesses a diverse scope and scale of data in order to write a book that strives for coherence and consistency despite its obvious limitations as a short, stand-alone text. This includes extensive use of original Japanese-language sources. These include the incorporation of, among other available materials, government reports, National Diet minutes, news media sources, interviews with selected stakeholders on the ground and a broad variety of secondary literature. The combined insights provided from this mixed-method approach offer an original perspective from which to consider why Okinawa continues to act as a specific, multifold locus for potential major power conflict. At the same time, they also open up new ground in terms of extending and developing a number of potential pathways towards the establishment of greater stability and prosperity.

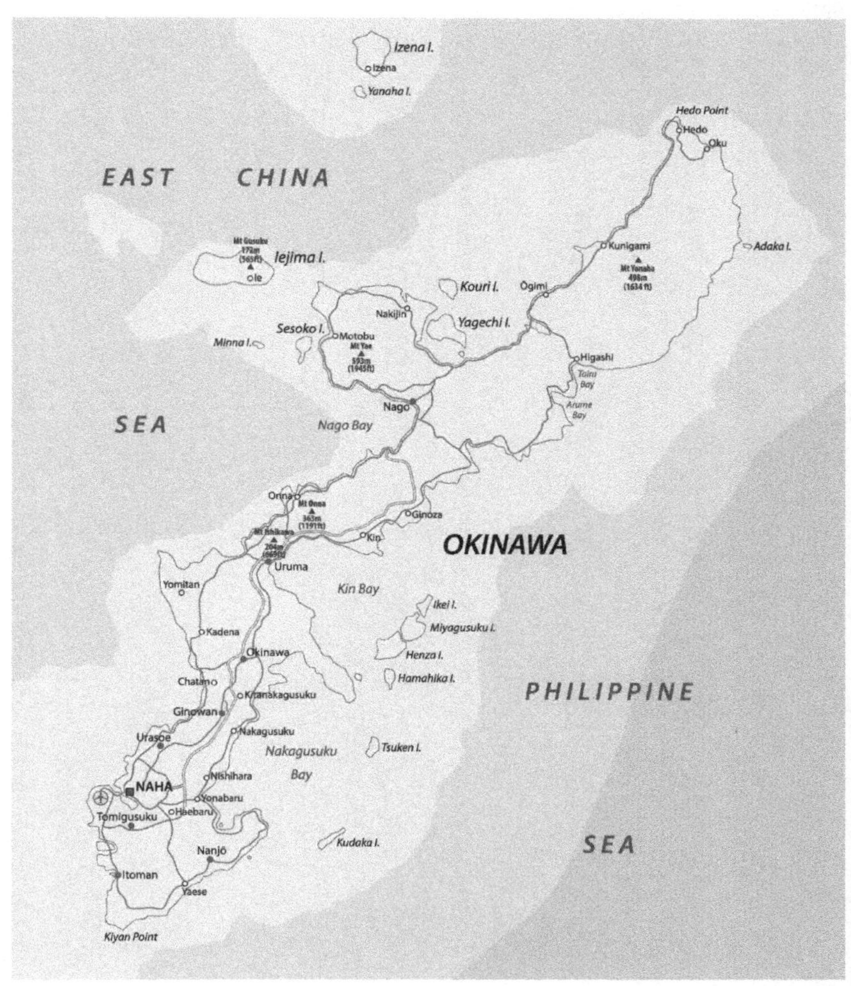

Map 1 Okinawa

Source: iStock.

Map 2 East Asia, showing Okinawa amid the contested East China Sea

Source: iStock

1

Introduction

Okinawa should be one of the most famous and popular destinations on the planet. As part of the Ryukyu Islands arc that stretches southwestward from the tip of Japan's southernmost main island, Kyushu, down almost as far as the northeast coast of Taiwan, Okinawa Prefecture sits amid the coral-filled, emerald-green waters that separate the East China Sea to the west and Pacific Ocean to the east (see Map 2). Yet its idyllic subtropical climate, rich fishing grounds and pacifistic local culture belie a deeply troubled past, strained present and ominous future. This is because Okinawa has historically been a flashpoint for great power rivalry and once again threatens to become one, in economic, political and geostrategic terms. The main island of Okinawa, its remote off-islands and their maritime surrounds are a site of unique geostrategic, socio-cultural, economic and environmental interest, but the islands' pivotal position has also previously made them a battleground and makes them a potential site of future conflict. This includes an ongoing contest for power and regional hegemony between the United States (US), its staunch ally in East Asia, Japan, and a rising China. In the past, the prefecture has progressed from being a vassal state of China in the form of an independent kingdom, to colonization by Japan, becoming a US protectorate after Japan's defeat in the Second World War, and then from 1972 to the present once again reverting to Japanese sovereign rule as Japan's forty-seventh prefecture.

There have been various significant developments since its reversion to Japanese rule, including how the prefecture has been affected by its disproportionate hosting of American – and now increasingly Japanese – armed forces stationed at the numerous US and Japan Self Defense Force (JSDF) military bases on the islands. The US presence in particular has increasingly become the focus of a broader regional power contest being played out between the US, China and Japan, with substantial interest also from Taiwan, both Koreas and Russia. Okinawa and the so-called First Island Chain, along which it is located, therefore, remain key sites of great power competition and contestation, making them a seemingly inevitable flashpoint in the coming decades of the twenty-first century.

This book, therefore, adopts a historically informed interdisciplinary approach to understand Okinawa from a set of intersecting and overlapping perspectives. In other words, it uses a variety of approaches to gain new insights. In so doing, it elucidates both the domestic and international dynamics of Okinawa's politics and political economy. This unpacks the puzzles and contradictions of Okinawan issues in terms of both resistance and acquiescence across the prefecture towards Japanese central government policies, the US presence and an increasingly assertive China. It undertakes this task by explicating the political, socio-economic and geostrategic divisions within contemporary Okinawa Prefecture, mostly as the result of internal competition and differing interests, as well as domination in key sectors by mainland actors. In turn, the divided politics and society of Okinawa are unveiled to explain the ability of the central government to perpetuate a degree of dominance over the prefecture and how this amplifies Okinawa's central position as a potential international flashpoint.

Ultimately, in the chapters that follow, I argue that the competing interests of the US, China and Japan over Okinawa and its surrounds, further complicated by Taiwan-related issues, the disputed Senkaku/Diaoyu islands (hereafter Senkaku)[1] and myriad complex domestic variables, are unstable and unsustainable in their current status quo. As a result, this makes these islands even more significant than often realized and deserving of much greater concerted attention than they have hitherto received, particularly in the academic English-language literature, global news media and mainstream Western policy-making circles. In

1 This volume takes no formal position on the Senkaku/Diaoyu/Tiaoyutai Islands dispute. Senkaku is used for brevity and relevance, given that this is how the islands are formally referred to from within Okinawa, rather than using the nominally neutral, historical term Pinnacle Islands.

response to this apparent gap in the extant literature, the book hereafter combines socio-economic, geopolitical and strategic military analyses into an in-depth, holistic analysis of Okinawa in order to evaluate the scale and scope of related risks and how they might be mitigated or countered. The enhanced significance of Okinawa's unique geostrategic positionality within the context of more commonly identified regional flashpoints, such as the Taiwan Strait and South China Sea, is thereby brought into focus so that a more integrated and nuanced understanding of the tensions and disputes of this key region can be gleaned.

A BRIEF HISTORY OF OKINAWA

Okinawa's islands have been inhabited by humans for more than 30 millennia, and although scientific opinion is divided on the origins and ethnicity of the early settlers, it is generally agreed that the Ryukyuan people represent an indigenous group, distinct from the Yamato people of mainland Japan. With this distinct ethnicity borne in mind, there are at least three things worthy of mention from Okinawan history that inform the analysis of contemporary Okinawa's development and transformation in economic, political and geostrategic terms. First, until subjugation by Japan's samurai-led feudal Satsuma clan in 1609, the multiple island groups that make up the Ryukyu Islands chain enjoyed a rich and diverse relationship with the surrounding great powers. This is illustrated by the fact that the Ryukyu Kingdom continued to make formal tribute missions to successive Chinese emperors until their annexation by Japan's Meiji government in 1879 (Matsumura 2015). These tributary relations illuminate not only the depth of historical ties with China but also the scope and scale of the Ryukyus' influence as a central trade and transit point between East and Southeast Asian nations (Matsuda 1967). Second, shortly before being forcibly annexed by Japan, including the de facto kidnapping and deportation to Tokyo of the islands' last king, Shō Tai, the Ryukyu Kingdom had concluded treaties of amity with the US, France and the Netherlands, thereby effectively formalizing interstate relations under nascent international law. The treaties would later be confiscated and destroyed by Japan's Meiji authorities, but they evidence the extent to which Okinawa has legitimate claims to self-determination and recognition as an independent political, economic and socio-cultural entity (Namihira 2014). The extended relevance of this becomes clearer as we explore how it has complicated issues of sovereignty and conflict centred on Okinawa today. Third, there is very little, if any, persuasive evidence to demonstrate that the Senkaku Islands were formally incorporated into the political bodies of Okinawa (previously Ryukyu), Japan or China before the Meiji government's designation of them as *terra nullius*, and later as an inherent part of Japan following victory against China in the first Sino-Japanese War of 1894–5 (Shaw 1999). Therefore, given the predatory nature of Japan vis-à-vis China in the conflict, including controversies over how the concluding postwar Treaty of Shimonoseki was negotiated and worded in Japan's favour as the victors, this has implications for how the Senkaku dispute is understood today by all relevant parties (Sato 2019: 51). More specifically, it is the vast discrepancy over differing interpretations of this history that is indeed central to what makes these islets a probable site of escalating conflict today (Pan 2007: 71).

In relation to the above, following a period of relative calm during the interwar period, Okinawa's extremely violent wartime history has done little, if anything, to reduce the intensity and complexity of how these "contested islands" (Hook 2015: 300), stretching more than 500 km from the Senkaku Islands to the Daito Islands, are competed over. Having been ruthlessly exploited by Tokyo's military rulers as Japan's *suteishi*, or throwaway stone, to blunt Allied advances across the Pacific – including through the confiscation of food, retributions against local residents and widespread sexual and physical abuse perpetrated by members of the Japanese Imperial Army (JIA) (McLauchlan 2014) – Okinawa succumbed to the only major land battle of the Pacific War fought on Japanese soil. This was the Battle of Okinawa, which came to be known as the "typhoon of steel" (Junkerman 2016a). The use of violent military force during this conflict, beyond anything mother nature regularly throws at the islands by way of tropical storms, tidal surges and earthquakes, saw the full ferocity of the US 10th Army let loose on Okinawa's Ie-Shima (now Ie-jima) Island, the Kerama Islands and Okinawa Main Island. Miyako Island was also shelled by the British Royal

Navy.[2] In the ensuing carnage, an estimated one-third, or some 150,000, of the entire civilian population were killed, either as a direct result of Allied shelling, starvation or group suicide, which was encouraged by the JIA to prevent capture (Okinawa Peace Memorial Museum 2022).

The US-led advance on Okinawa finally prevailed after almost three months of bloody fighting, following formal surrender by JIA forces on 21 June 1945, by which time the Battle of Okinawa had become the bloodiest of the Pacific War. It included some 90,000 Japanese military casualties taken in addition to the more than 150,000 civilian deaths already noted, as well as over 48,000 lost souls on the American side and massive losses of equipment at sea as Japan used *kamikaze* tactics against Allied ships in a desperate, and ultimately futile, attempt to repel one of the largest naval attack fleets ever assembled. In the battle's aftermath, thousands of Okinawans were interned in prison camps, where they suffered further physical and sexual abuse at the hands of fiercely anti-Japanese, war weary and unsympathetic male American troops (Karimata 2003). US forces were generally unaware of, or indifferent to, the fact that the local population had been as much a victim of wartime Japanese aggression as they were. Okinawans were severely discriminated against by mainland Japanese, often perceived as savages or second-class citizens despite their formal assimilation into the national body of Japan. This prejudice meant locals were regularly accused of being traitors and deserters by the JIA. In contrast, despite committing numerous atrocities and war crimes during and after the battle itself, Okinawa's new American colonizers did at least provide extensive welfare and infrastructural support. The island's shattered society and economy was thereafter rebuilt under the pretext of being a US overseas protectorate, complete with a new currency (the B-Dollar), education system and basic social welfare provisions (Ikeda 2003: 128).

In the decades that followed, Okinawan society was transformed, albeit at the mercy of its occupiers, who used the island as an "unsinkable aircraft carrier" to store weapons and station troops in preparation for dispatch to Cold War proxy wars that were to be fought in Korea,

2 Details of why the British limited their invasion of Miyako to a sea-based bombardment were provided by prospective mayoral candidate Daisuke Nagahama during an interview, 12 April 2023.

Vietnam and elsewhere (Kobayashi 2013: 2). As a result, the local economy became heavily reliant upon the disproportionately large number of US military bases for employment, industrial investment and hard currency. The monetary aspect primarily took the form of income from consumption of goods and services, such as tourism and the (mostly illegal) sex trade (Figal 2012: 28). This resulted in a growing power imbalance manifest between local residents and American servicemembers, who remained largely unaccountable for the felonies and misdemeanours they committed on the islands. These included heinous crimes such as hit-and-run road accidents, robbery and sexual violence (Robinson 2015: 46). The US military presence also caused severe environmental damage to rivers, soils and seas, some of which retain their toxicity to this day, as they became polluted with industrial run-off and toxic chemicals such as agent orange and polyfluoroalkyl substances.[3]

Okinawa's postwar experience in these regards needs to be contextualized in relation to, and in contrast with, that of the Japanese mainland. After a relatively short period of American US occupation and administration under the General Headquarters of Supreme Command of Allied Powers from August 1945, Japan restored full sovereignty following conclusion of the 1951 Treaty of San Francisco and its implementation in the following year. Land reforms, socio-economic restructuring and massive levels of external investment then propelled the country into a period of extended high growth and increasing prosperity. This spurred Okinawan pro-reversion movements to grow in strength and purpose, as the islanders aspired to become *hondo nami*, or "in line", with the status and lifestyle of mainland Japan (Maeshiro 2021: 389). The political elements of these movements took the form of both peaceful and non-peaceful demonstrations, ultimately culminating in the Koza uprising of 1970 that saw US military vehicles burned and overturned. Thereafter, as Washington sought to cut the rising costs associated with prosecuting its protracted wars in Vietnam and elsewhere, the push for Okinawa's reversion gained new impetus on economic as well as social grounds. In other words, Okinawans' desire to be rid of occupying American forces aligned with the US State Department's prerogative to transfer the burdensome costs of social welfare and infrastructure on

3 Interview with former Itoman City Office staff, 1 February 2023.

Okinawa from Washington to Tokyo. Okinawa duly reverted to Japanese rule in 1972, on condition that the US be allowed to retain all its military facilities on the Ryukyu Islands and be paid an *omoiyari yosan*, or "sympathy budget", from Japan's tax coffers to maintain them (Okinawa Times 2022a). This also meant that the Senkaku Islands, which had been assigned "residual sovereignty" in 1951 under provisions of the San Francisco Treaty, were effectively returned to direct Japanese control and officially administered from within Okinawa Prefecture by Ishigaki City.

Despite these seemingly mutually beneficial developments, tensions and resentment between Okinawa, the Government of Japan (GoJ) and the US military remain to this day. This is primarily as a function of imbalanced power relations and the unequal burden of military bases and their associated risks shouldered by the prefecture and its inhabitants. Not least, in spite of Okinawa's restored legal status as a full prefecture of Japan, the Ryukyu Islands continue to host over 70 per cent of the country's American military bases, which occupy almost 20 per cent of the prefecture's total area that is itself only 0.6 per cent of Japan's total land mass. Consequentially, the deleterious behaviour of US service members, who often have little understanding of, or empathy towards, the local community and its culture, has continued, as has resistance and anger towards them. These elements reached a crisis point in 1995 when, after a catalogue of escalating, unpunished crimes had been endured by islanders over a period of decades, three US Marines abducted and raped a 12-year-old Okinawan school girl. The servicemembers involved were from Marine Corps Air Station (MCAS) Futenma, which, coupled with being the site of numerous deadly accidents as a result of its location in the middle of the populous city of Ginowan, is in flagrant breach of legal restrictions that would normally apply to such facilities when constructed on US home soil. This includes the base having no clearance zone around its perimeter fence, so schools, hospitals and an international university, as well as residential buildings, all back directly onto the base. Within this context, the fallout from the incidence of child rape led to unprecedented demonstrations and an agreement by Washington and Tokyo to return MCAS Futenma, as the "the world's most dangerous base", to Okinawan administrative control (Lummis 2018). The deal reached, however, was ultimately only agreed to on condition that a replacement facility be built further north at Henoko Bay, which sits atop a pristine coral reef surrounded by seas containing rare endangered wildlife species that migrate to and from its fragile *inō*, or tidal plain.

Since the conception of this replacement facility, which actually dates back to a clandestine plan drawn up in the 1960s for a new airstrip on the site, construction of the new base at Henoko has faced fierce resistance from anti-base campaigners and environmentalists alike (Japan Times 2016). This includes popular opposition from across the prefecture as well as through the courts by the Okinawa Prefectural Government, albeit under constant threat of counter-litigation and targeting by the GoJ. As a result, work on the new facility has been stalled and intermittent since the late 1990s. However, the prefectural authorities have increasingly been subjected to litigation by the national government in Tokyo, who appear bent on setting a precedent in response to Okinawa's local government leading and coordinating efforts to prevent completion of the project throughout the first quarter of the twenty-first century (Abe 2021). The base remains less than half complete at the time of writing, although the GoJ has moved to initiate land reclamation on the second half of the proposed landing strips in the bay, after forcing through a legal decision that rejected the local authority's claims that the seabed of the site was unsuitable for undersea construction of the base's runways. However, the issue is exacerbated by the fact that the new facility is paid for by Japanese rather than US taxpayers, meaning that the American military are relatively satisfied with the present arrangement of operating out of MCAS Futenma for no extra cost, placing the onus on the GoJ to see the project through to completion. This therefore pits the GoJ against Okinawa Prefecture, rather than the US side being engaged with directly.

In response, Tokyo's ruling Liberal Democratic Party (LDP) continues to work closely with its counterparts in Washington to present a unified front in the name of national security (Mason 2023). This maintains the position that the new base is essential for the purposes of regional deterrence, claiming that despite an agreement to return MCAS Futenma, this cannot be implemented until the "replacement" facility is built at Henoko (O'Shea 2019). Simply put, the LDP promulgates the narrative that citizens must choose between security on the one hand, or environmental and social protection on the other, despite the fact that there is little evidence to suggest that both cannot be achieved simultaneously. Meanwhile, American and Japanese forces have intensified their focus to the Southwest Island Chain, which incorporates the assumption that Okinawa is a probable flashpoint for confrontation with China. This includes advancing integrated military systems to enable greater interoperability of the two militaries, as well as the construction of a series of new JSDF facilities on outlying Okinawan islands. These have now already been built, and in some cases upgraded, on Miyako Island, Ishigaki Island (which retains administration of the Senkaku Islands) and Yonaguni Island, within physical sight of Taiwan.

A DENSELY POPULATED, PRISTINE CORAL PARADISE

As with Okinawa Main Island, the three key outlying islands noted above, which form part of the Sakishima and Yaeyama clusters (see Map 3),[4] respectively, are not mere rocky outcrops being utilized as strategic bases amid great power competition. They are home to a staggeringly beautiful natural environment, as well as sizeable populations. The prefecture as a whole is home to almost 1.5 million people and is one of the very few prefectures in Japan where the population is relatively young and actually increasing in number. Within this total, Miyako Island and Ishigaki Island boast around 50,000 residents each, with Yonaguni Island now increasing its population to just under 2,000 as a result of newly stationed JSDF forces and their families having migrated onto the island to staff the new reconnaissance base. This marks an upturn after it had declined slowly to just under 1,300 inhabitants, primarily because the US and Japanese governments enforced the breaking-off of direct trade routes to nearby Taiwan. At the time of writing, with seven fully accredited universities, multiple world-class professional

4 Other inhabited outlying Okinawan islands include the extremely remote Daito Islands, as well as those to the west of Okinawa Main Island, such as Kume-Jima, Tonaki-Jima, Aguni-Jima and the Iheya-Izena cluster, but none of these are generally considered as being as strategically significant as those running along the First Island Chain itself, hence the absence of military bases on them.

sports facilities, dual-use international airports and seaports, including airports on all of the islands listed above and some of their further off-islands, Okinawa is highly connected and integral to the regional economy. It is also a society that is more reminiscent in many ways of small independent states in Europe than the kind of slow, simple way and pace of life often associated with other Pacific islands and outposts (Miyauchi 2016: 33).

Despite this dramatic demographic and infrastructural contrast with other comparable land masses, the islands' physical environment is every bit as, if not more, spectacular than Hawaii, Guam and other regional hubs that also suffer from increasing pollution, overfishing and the mass disposal of marine waste. Okinawa's unique subtropical ecosystem is, however, likewise equally under threat. Marine inhabitants include endangered species of sea turtle, dugong and subtropical

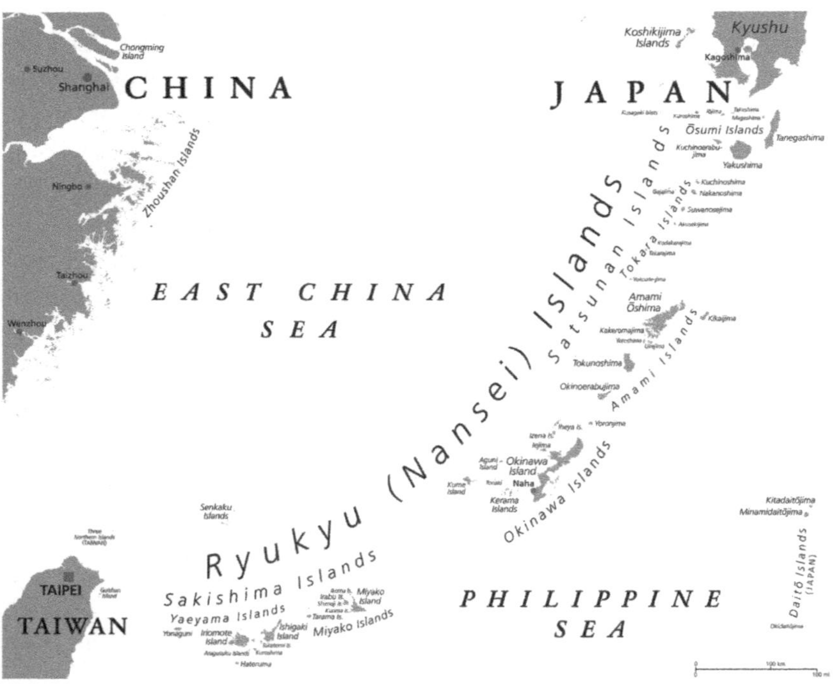

Map 3 Okinawa amid the First and Second Island Chains

Source: iStock.

fish, which all rely on ancient live coral beds that stretch the distance of the island chain and are complemented by rarely observed on-land lifeforms, such as the Yanbaru rail, forest frogs, tube-nosed bats and spider crabs. In this regard, the unique ecosystem is another key aspect of Okinawa as a flashpoint, in the sense that it is not just a strategically significant location but is also emblematic of the kinds of global processes that have resulted in the widespread destruction of coral reefs and fragile ecosystems across the planet. These are directly affected by the powerful states and commercial actors who disregard their intrinsic value in the pursuit of geopolitical or economic incentives (Palz 2021).

This environmental struggle has been the subject of multiple international court hearings. All of these have ruled, albeit in a non-binding form, against construction of the new base designated by the GoJ as the replacement facility for MCAS Futenma, which extends into the virgin ocean from the existing Camp Schwab facility across the adjacent Henoko and Oura bays. In spite of this, and the evident factuality of base construction atop a pristine coral reef amounting to an environmental holocaust, Japan's judiciary has consistently worked in lockstep with the GoJ to obstruct and legally penalize efforts by the Prefectural Government to prevent the project on ecological and conservational grounds (Greenpeace 2016). Amid this, while the addition of a small group of activists that have joined anti-base protests at Henoko and elsewhere on Okinawa in some ways works to raise the profile of the issues at hand, they also complicate and increase the number of factors and actors that might be involved in any potential conflict. In addition, their emphasis on ecological issues in one sense dilutes the focus of local opposition, because other protestors are objecting on political and socio-economic, rather than environmental, grounds. In other words, the majority of Okinawan protestors are primarily opposed to the presence of the US military in terms of their violation of human rights, sovereignty and risks posed to inhabitants, rather than the environmental hazards that they cause. Nevertheless, the combined logrolling of politically and environmentally motivated forces does create significant agency in terms of tempering what would otherwise probably become the unbridled fortification, and concretization, of the islands.

DISPUTED ISLANDS AND GAPS IN THE LITERATURE

As the discussion above reveals, and the following chapters explore, the history, politics, economics, society and environment of Okinawa are all contested spheres. In response, this book attempts to straddle several bodies of academic literature in order to provide a balanced, interdisciplinary perspective, which illustrates, rather than avoids, Okinawa's complexities. This means situating the text amid traditional International Relations (IR) (Chen & Shimizu 2019; O'Shea 2019), international political economy (Tanji & Broudy 2017), politics (Egami 1994; Nishiyama 2022), history (Namihira 2014; Akamine 2017) and area studies (Bazhenova & Goriacheva 2023) accounts, among other more seminal transdisciplinary works (Figal 2012; Matsumura 2015). Such an approach inevitably means charting a challenging course between competing theoretical and ideological standpoints. However, the aim is to adopt an eclectic examination of the complex issues discussed. Indeed, only through this broader lens can we hope to provide an enhanced degree of meaningful understanding, which draws on these differing approaches while also addressing some of the specific concerns and points of conflict that they are yet to satisfactorily resolve. To this end, it is first necessary to assess the current status quo. This includes current points of dispute within the literature on, and surrounding, the Okinawan islands and how these have been framed by leading scholars in the field.

If American bases on Okinawa increase the potential for both domestic and interstate conflict, then one can certainly argue credibly that the disputed Senkaku Islands are, for the foreseeable future, the most likely location for armed conflict between China and Japan, and China and the US–Japan alliance, to actually occur (Costa 2017).[5]

5 The complexities of this likelihood are discussed in greater depth in later chapters, but it is worth noting here that there are two separate and probable triggers that could turn Okinawa into a flashpoint. The first is direct confrontation over the Senkaku Islands, probably as the result of Japanese (and US) responses to a Chinese incursion or other provocation into either the maritime sphere or airspace. The second is as the result of China needing to disable US aerial capabilities on Okinawa in order to prevent American defence of Taiwan. In other words, prior to Beijing ordering an invasion directed at Taipei, it would

Furthermore, the dynamic status quo, involvement of grey-zone actors such as armed paramilitaries and heavily armed coastguards and fishing ships, as well as the geographical remoteness of these rocky outcrops, means that any escalation might rapidly spiral out of control (see Map 3).[6] This could include the exchange of deadly fire between autonomous or semi-autonomous combatants before government authorities or state militaries can respond effectively through formal political and diplomatic channels, although experts are divided on exactly what form those responses would take. In recent years, the situation has developed into a precarious standoff; the very real dangers of which can be estimated in qualitative and quantitative terms (O'Shea 2015). In addition to bombastic rhetoric from both Japanese and Chinese parties regarding ownership and governance of these uninhabited islets, the number of days where incursions from unauthorized fishing boats and other vessels occurred reached a peak of 334 in the calendar year of 2022 and remained an almost daily occurrence throughout 2023, although how these incursions are defined and categorized is also the subject of heated debate (Sato & Chadha 2022), much of which lacks deeper contextualization within the broader issues of Okinawa's politics, economics and security. Hence, the current volume contributes towards filling this gap in the literature by providing a more holistic analysis in those regards. The urgency is further highlighted by both Japan and China investing heavily in armour and deadly weaponry with which to equip their respective coastguards in what has become a de facto arms race between officially non-military arms of government (Takahashi 2018). Furthermore, recent legal changes, particularly those enacted by the authorities in Beijing, effectively authorize the use of lethal force should these now powerfully armoured coastguard fleets engage in direct conflict (Asia Maritime Transparency Initiative 2021).

Indeed, as argued by more pessimistic scholars (Sato 2019), China now has multiple and unpredictable variables at play that might spark

---

probably launch missile attacks against US bases on Okinawa to secure the surrounding area and debilitate Taiwan's would-be allies.

6 MOFA emphasizes these concerns through its official position on the Senkaku Islands, as detailed in a 13 December 2022 online statement, as well as through its documenting of the number of Chinese incursions into the area.

such an escalation. Aside from the more obvious historical claims and anti-Japanese sentiment within Chinese society, these include use of the Senkaku Islands as an internal political bargaining chip. Thereby aspiring Chinese leadership contenders might seek to demonstrate their prowess vis-à-vis their domestic rivals through wrestling control of this contested maritime space from Japan. In other words, in an environment in which rising through the ranks of the Chinese Communist Party (CCP) and Peoples Liberation Army (PLA) relies upon public and intra-party demonstrations of strength, seizing dominion over what has now become a high-profile and domestically almost universally agreed upon dispute through charismatic and unwavering leadership offers a viable means to career success.[7] Similarly, on the Japanese side, nationalization of the Senkaku Islands, in tandem with a more proactive and robust regional foreign policy in the security sphere, has reinforced Japan's resolute position that the Senkaku chain and its surrounding waters are unequivocally sovereign Japanese territory (MOFA 2022). Yet here, too, the significance of Okinawa within such a process of contestation, despite having deep historical ties to the Asian mainland (Namihira 2014), is largely overlooked or underplayed by contemporary scholarship. This is compounded by the intensifying US–Japan integration and interoperability of security forces that are focused on a broader pivot to Japan's Southwest Island Chain. The chain, marked by a loosely and somewhat ambiguously demarcated line of islands, includes the heavily inhabited landmasses noted above, such as Okinawa's main island, as well as a plethora of uninhabited islets and outcrops. The Senkaku Islands' contested position just inside the chain complicates matters further, as does the US's somewhat contradictory position that it will defend the islands under Article 5 of the US–Japan Security Alliance should they be invaded, but that it will not take a formal position on the sovereignty of the same rocks (CRS Service Report 2021: 2).

7 This kind of aggressive foreign policy stance taken by aspiring Chinese diplomats, military leaders and lawmakers, known collectively as "wolf warrior diplomacy", has potentially very significant implications for how Okinawa and its related geopolitical issues are approached by Beijing, particularly given that this approach is championed by the CCP leadership, including Premier Xi Jinping; see Lau (2022).

This leaves a fragile, dynamic and seemingly unsustainable status quo that has not been comprehensively addressed by the extant literature, especially in terms of the significance of, and complex role played by, Okinawa. And while substantive military analyses of potential conflict over the Senkaku cluster suggest a combined US–Japan military force could currently comfortably repel any concerted aggression by the People's Liberation Army Navy (PLAN), such assessments rarely incorporate comprehensive estimations of China's grey-zone activities (Bartok 2022). These include armed fishing boats, navy-strength coastguard ships and other paramilitary vessels. Moreover, current military analyses do not satisfactorily explain battle procedure or de-escalation scenarios should a lethal exchange of force occur between the respective coastguards, which are not part of either state's formal military or security forces. In these regards, the chapters that follow address this analytical gap by mapping out the underlying causes and broader implications of such conflict from a holistic perspective, incorporating a wide range of interdisciplinary data and in-depth analysis.

SOURCES FOR INVESTIGATION

The book examines a cross-section of relevant mixed-source data, which include extensive use of original Japanese-language materials. It therein draws on a broad variety of qualitative and quantitative sources in order to investigate the nature, likelihood and extent of Okinawa as a potential regional flashpoint between great powers, and what might be done to counter such an ominous status. In order to embed and contextualize the original empirical content within existing scholarship, as outlined above, the investigation begins with a comprehensive interrogation and incorporation of key ideas from the leading literature in the field. Indeed, one of the central goals of the book is to highlight the pits and fissures already noted in scholarly debate on Okinawa, while also seeking to supplement these through a synthesis of the many insightful analyses of the islands and their surrounds that are available across the social science disciplines. This scholarly foundation is built upon through an application of the range of primary and secondary data sources alluded to above. These include a diverse intersection of news media reports, professional journalists' accounts, governmental and bureaucratic documents, museum entries, local authority publications, commercial business releases and available corporate information. A group of semi-structured interviews from field research conducted on Okinawa, which were targeted at specific key stakeholders identified with related Okinawan issues, provide additional, valuable insights.

This multi-source cross-section of data allows a flexible interpretive approach that facilitates a hitherto unprecedented research method in relation to Okinawa. Simply put, it means that we can bring together a variety of interrelated concepts and issues for discussion in one book, where previously they had been separated or addressed in isolation. More specifically, by critically examining such a broad range and diversity of sources across, for example, military security, political and socio-economic spheres, it becomes possible to highlight the many contradictions and contestations that they contain. At the same time, by demonstrating their interconnectivity, it brings to the fore areas for potential cooperation and constructive dialogue. In other words, this analytical framework tells the story of what is happening on Okinawa and why through one combined narrative. Concretely, through analysis of the pertaining discourse, it joins up the dots between high politics, economics and security, on the one hand, and people's lives and natural environment, on the other. For instance, it links together discussions that focus on Okinawa and its surrounds about nationalism, regionalism, arms, big business and social identity. This includes crosspollination between those who are, among other things: both for and against greater fortification of Okinawa; those seeking to prioritize the islands' pristine marine environment and those trying to exploit it; those working to leverage maximum commercial gain from Okinawa Prefecture's limited resources and how they are defined; those committed to developing key main island sites as a locus for scientific and sporting excellence; those who wish to preserve or conserve more traditional ways of life, as well as those who identify as being Okinawan before Japanese and vice versa.

STRUCTURE OF THE BOOK: THREE FOCUS POINTS FOR A MULTIFACETED FLASHPOINT

This opening chapter has set the stage, then, for a renewed urgency in investigating Okinawa as a flashpoint. It has also put forward a broad framework for how this can be achieved through the examination of diverse interdisciplinary data sources. This has revealed the necessity for detailed, integrated analysis of a range of factors affecting Okinawa's security, governmental administration, regionally embedded market and historically distinct society. All of these areas contain potential friction points that could lead to greater instability or conflict at various key intersections across this geographically and culturally dispersed prefecture. Amid this, the Senkaku Islands, formally administered from Okinawa's Ishigaki Island, have been identified as a site of particular and growing concern with regard to escalating tensions between several of the world's greatest powers. The paragraphs below detail how these issues are to be tackled systematically through the analysis of a series of distinct yet interlinked sectors that make up the core chapters of the book.

Chapter 2 contains a condensed explanation and analysis of Okinawa's current domestic politics. After first detailing the structure of policy formation and implementation on the islands, this includes explicating how local issues are embedded within a complex national and international political environment. The discussion unearths insights into myriad significant contradictions that exacerbate the prefecture's precarious position. These range from the vastly different political narratives of *security* being told by the US, China, Japan and Okinawa Prefectural Government, through to Okinawa's pacifist-led fight for environmental protection and the majority of its islanders' prerogatives to improve the prefectural economy. It also focuses on how attention to, and the political prioritization of, these diverse issues and their related efforts are significantly affected by variables such as demography, geographical location and identity. In addition, the chapter articulates Okinawans' contradicting desire to be covered by the US–Japan Security Alliance in order to protect them against perceived fears of Chinese expansion, while at the same time wanting to reduce the number and scale of military bases on Okinawa to avoid heinous crimes committed by American servicemembers and the pollution of local ecosystems. Closer examination also reveals a contest of political ideologies and disputed ideas over how best to minimize the threat of these facilities being targeted by rival states such as China and North Korea.

Building on Chapter 2 from an economic standpoint, Chapter 3 traces the money trail to expose the competing commercial interests at play in the conflict over Okinawa's base economy and outer off-islands. This illuminates the historical reasons behind the current status of US forces on the Ryukyu Islands and the financial incentives provided for them and JSDF personnel to be stationed throughout Okinawa. Close examination points to the primacy of three core industries – namely construction, tourism and military bases – as being central to the structure and, in one sense, economic colonization of the prefecture by powerful mainland Japanese and American vested interests. It also assesses the economically driven aspects of both local Okinawan authorities' and their Chinese counterparts' policy prerogatives. These include a critique of Beijing's claims to the Senkaku Islands only after oil was discovered beneath the surrounding seabed and Okinawa's reversion to Japan had been agreed. Contrastingly, the influence of Japan's national government in providing a "sympathy budget", or *omoiyari yosan*, to financially support American troops stationed on Okinawa, as well as its massive domestic aid package in the form of special lump sum payments to local government, is further examined. Particular attention is afforded here to the impact these funding practices have upon local development and self-autonomy, as well as broader regional dynamics by extension.

In developing core strands of the discussion of the preceding two chapters, Chapter 4 contextualizes the intersection of political economy and geostrategic security by returning to examine Okinawa as the "keystone of the Pacific". This is documented amid an emerging great power contest over the Indo-Pacific's security architecture. It includes an explanation of the strategic significance of Okinawa to the US–Japan alliance and how it is increasingly playing host to the intensified interoperability of American and Japanese forces throughout the Southwest Island Chain. This is engaged with through a substantive assessment of the importance of Okinawa's proximity to Taiwan and the impact of new JSDF facilities on outer islands, as well as a re-evaluation of the security status quo around and in the skies above the waters of the Senkaku

Islands. The latter element encompasses possible scenarios for how the tense situation might be escalated or deescalated, in addition to how these relate to tensions over the South China Sea and Taiwan Straits, as China continues to increase its security capabilities relative to those of Japan and the US.

In conclusion, Chapter 5 brings together the major strands of socio-political, economic and security-based arguments to reinforce the scope and gravity of contemporary issues on Okinawa and put forward tentative proposals for policy actions in response. These are shown to be worthy of closer scrutiny in the context of the islands becoming a flashpoint between major powers with significant regional, and potentially global, ramifications. As the concluding chapter, this details the relevance of how the various aspects and elements discussed throughout the chapters outlined above interact, emphasizing their connectivity and inextricable linkage. Ultimately, it argues that by pursuing narrowly defined and inflexibly conceptualized interests the leading actors and stakeholders involved are driving forwards an escalating and unsustainable dynamic that threatens regional security. This leads to a high, but not inevitable, probability of great power conflict in one form or another, as detailed in a final series of short scenarios. However, these include a constructive discussion of how the ultimate flashpoint scenario can – with wise leadership, localized innovations and popular support – be avoided. As such, it offers a blueprint for the positive future of Okinawa's potential-rich but precariously positioned paradise islands.

2

Social identities, pacifism and power politics

OKINAWA'S COMPLEX POLITICAL STRUCTURE

Okinawa's political make-up is complicated. As such, in priming the discussion for further development of the respective economic and security-based arguments made in Chapters 3 and 4, this chapter makes the central argument that complex domestic political divisions are likely to become pivotal in relation to Okinawa manifesting itself as a potential flashpoint. More specifically, it details how these divisions intersect with ideology, identity, demographics and geographical location in a form that means each of these variables has a significant effect upon related policies affecting the prefecture and its surrounds as a whole. In order to fully understand their interrelated dynamics, however, we must once again review the historical antecedents of contemporary Okinawan politics, as many core aspects rooted in the past remain pivotal to the present operation of Okinawan local authorities and the larger political structures of which they form a key part.

Formal assimilation, which took the form of a de facto annexation through *shobun*, or disposition, of the Ryukyu Kingdom by Japan's Meiji rulers, was officially completed in 1879. After this, on the face of it, Okinawa became one of the 47 standardized Japanese prefectures. These are administrative units with highly limited self-autonomy, somewhere between the status of a US state and a British county. This should have meant equal treatment under the Meiji constitution and no more or less self-autonomy than any of the other 46 equivalent local authorities. However, the unique history of the Ryukyu Kingdom, along with mainland Japanese discrimination towards Okinawans, as well as residual Chinese interest and inter-island competition within the prefecture, meant that political wrangling continued up to the point of Japan's entry into the Pacific War. At that time, rapidly deteriorating regional international relations acted to accelerate Tokyo's turn towards militarism, leading to the centralized authorities taking authoritarian control over Okinawa and using the islands as their *suteishi*, or throwaway stones, with which to defend the Japanese main islands from the impending Allied onslaught.

As alluded to in Chapter 1, and detailed further below, this led to gross violations of human rights and the complete removal of most Okinawans from any kind of meaningful political participation in the governance of their prefecture. Despite facing the largest proportional casualties of any prefecture in the war itself, in a cruel twist of irony, meaningful citizenship was also largely denied to most of Okinawa's residents even after implementation of the US-drafted postwar constitution, on account of Okinawa becoming a US protectorate under military rule. This meant that rather than being returned to the restructured and rapidly democratizing national political body of a Japan that was soon to be sovereign again, Okinawans were left comparatively impoverished and politically powerless. The islands were thrown into a state of limbo.

What is perhaps most striking, however, is the legacy of Okinawa's unique political history in this regard. Even following formal reversion to Japanese rule in 1972, Okinawa has retained a large number of unusual legal provisions and bureaucratic entities that do not exist in, or are distinct from, other prefectures of Japan. These relate mostly to provisions surrounding the politically delicate status and operation of US military bases on the islands, but they also serve as a means by which the central authorities in Tokyo can keep particularly tight control over prefectural and other local authorities (Okubo 2009).

This includes the manipulation of budgets to both incentivize good, or compliant, behaviour by the Okinawan Prefectural Government and punish its opposition to any central government policies, including the construction of controversial military bases, such as the replacement facility for MCAS Futenma at Henoko highlighted in Chapter 1. These political levers are in addition to the use of extra-governmental bodies, also unique to the prefecture, such as the Okinawan Bureau of General Affairs (formally an arm of the Cabinet Office) and the Okinawa Defense Bureau, which act as a buffer against localized resistance and dissent.

These bureaucratic subdivisions also oversee coordinating internal security forces and act as an intermediary between the judiciary, US military organizations stationed on Okinawa and the Okinawa Prefectural authorities, all on behalf of central government. In other words, extra layers of bureaucracy ensure that any local political movements and initiatives on Okinawa are limited in their power and scope to enact real change. Conversely, the system effectively embeds powerful governmental actors in positions where they can work to retain the political status quo in favour of the ruling party. In the post-reversion era, aside from a handful of tumultuous years of opposition rule, this has meant sustained domination by the LDP.

The current structures of governance on Okinawa, therefore, resemble a layered cake where Okinawan political agency is kept very much spread and squashed at the bottom and has highly limited ability to alter, even incrementally, a mostly rigid status quo. This is sustained as a result of uniform national educational practices, bureaucratic centralized control and *gaiatsu*, or external US pressure. As such, the current political structure of complex interlocking layers can be represented approximately as a configuration of interacting sites and levels of authority (see Figure 2.1). However, in addition to the external interests and influences already alluded to, Okinawa's politics of today are also deeply embedded within, and bound up with, discord between successive generations and their complex identities. These are manifest in the rapid changes experienced through the transformation from feudal kingdom to advanced modern society.

CONTESTED GENERATIONAL AND SPATIAL IDENTITIES AS A CAUSE OF CONFLICT

Okinawa has sustained a powerful pacifist identity in one form or another since its unification as the single Ryukyu Kingdom almost seven centuries ago. As a political stance, this has mostly been manifested as a resistant response to central government pressures, belligerence from various internal and external actors, and meddling from foreign powers (Akamine 2017: 9). Those of a more cynical disposition, meanwhile, might claim that Okinawa's leading political figures and renowned

Okinawa within the international system of states

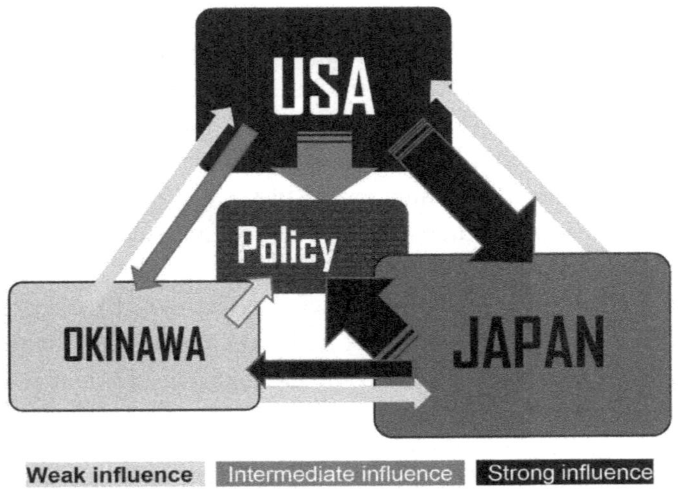

Okinawa within Japan's domestic political system

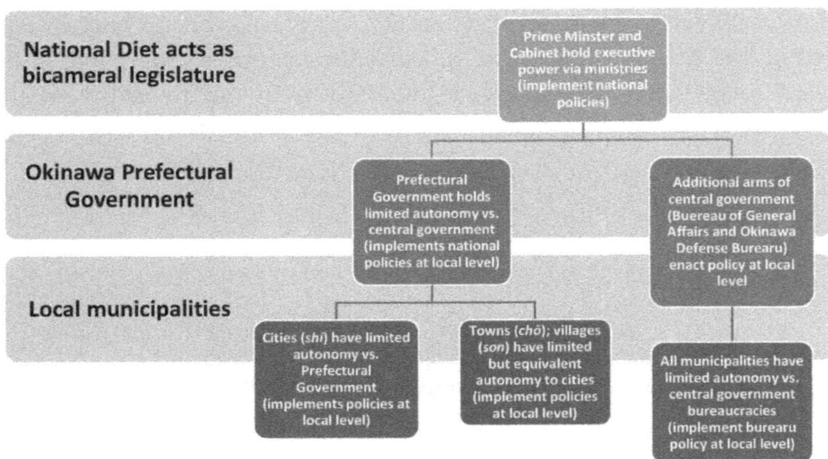

Figure 2.1 Okinawa's complex political structure

Source: Compiled by the author.

thinkers have deliberately played great powers off against each other in order to manipulate a framing of victimized circumstances and thereby leverage an advantage in terms of gaining political and economic concessions.[1] If that were the case, such tactics have surely been justified, given the islands' precarious position sandwiched between some of the world's greatest powers, including at times of war and extreme violence. The fact that Okinawans, and Okinawa as a whole, has been able to sustain and project an antimilitarist local identity despite the enormous pressures brought to bear upon its politics and society by Japan, the US and China is testimony to the islanders' unbreakable *tamashii*, or enduring spirit, and resolve amid a conflict-prone international neighbourhood full of larger peer-competitors (Nagayama 2023).

However, in recent years, as central government authorities, mainstream commercial news outlets and social media platforms have emphasized Japan's supposedly "unprecedentedly rapidly deteriorating regional security environment",[2] a number of competing and often contradicting narratives have emerged that are reshaping Okinawan opinions and political identity. Particularly since the end of the Cold War, broadly speaking, this has seen the rise of a more conservative and nationalist youth sentiment among those who are politically active (Mason 2019: 191). At the same time, political apathy, particularly among so-called Generation X and Millennial cohorts, has also been an increasing trend that contributes to the erosion of local identity. Younger generations increasingly define their socio-political status and positionality in relation to globalized commercial markets and individual patterns of consumption, rather than solely through ties to kinship or locality. In that regard, these competing contemporary identities contribute to Okinawa's identification as a flashpoint because they are deeply divisive along generational, locational and occupational lines. Moreover, they are all aspects that intersect with national and international policy trajectories.

---

1 A particularly controversial proponent of this idea was former US Japan Bureau Chief Kevin Maher; see McCurry (2011).

2 This is included in the Japan MOD's official policy documents, including the "Bōeishō no seisaku" [MOD policy] posted on its homepage.

Here, the nature of these socio-political intersections is interrogated within the context of great power rivalries, specifically in terms of how these exert extended influence on the islands and their inhabitants, as well as the impact of a broader national decline in Japan's postwar pacifist social norms (Hook *et al.* 2011: 77). Therein, at every level of analysis, from the international to the local, politicized narratives are shown to be key elements in directing related policy outcomes. This is because each sphere is both interconnected and contested, from military bases to environmental protection and economic growth. An examination of these sites of contestation, therefore, reveals why they represent contributing factors in Okinawa's status as a probable future site for multifold forms of violent conflict. First, in order to properly frame and understand the depth of the problems at hand, a deeper dive into postwar Okinawan history and politics needs to be further contextualized beyond what we have already covered. This is in terms of both the linkages between the key events outlined in Chapter 1 and the legacies of the Ryukyu Kingdom noted above.

POSTWAR TO THE PRESENT

"Postwar" is itself a contested concept. However, putting definitional issues to one side, let us begin with a closer examination of the Battle of Okinawa in order to provide the relevant context for what was to follow in the period after the physical devastation that vanquished the main island and its surrounds (Feifer 2001: 1). From the summer of 1942 the US military and its allies slowly turned the tide on what had been one of the fastest and largest geomilitary expansions in human history by the Imperial Japanese Army (IJA) across the Asia-Pacific. After a series of now famous successes in island-hopping across the western Pacific, from Guadalcanal to Iwo Jima, the Allies ultimately identified Okinawa as the "keystone of the Pacific" in terms of being the key site from which to launch a full-scale invasion of Japan. Realizing the strategic importance of this southwest island outpost, the US led the largest American armada in history to attack what was by then a heavily fortified set of IJA defensive positions, obliterating much of the island and killing over a third of its inhabitants in the process. Okinawans who could not or would not leave their homes were subject to a horrendous bombardment by the maritime Allied forces of the US 5th Fleet, as well as widespread confiscation of land and food by the desperate IJA defenders. These members of Japan's 32nd Army, rather than attempting to defend civilians as Japanese citizens, treated Okinawa, as noted, as a *suteishi* and its inhabitants as spies and foreigners in their own land.

Hence, after being abused by the IJA tasked to defend them and obliterated by the US-led Allied invasion during the Battle of Okinawa throughout the springtime of 1945, it is unsurprising that after the battle there were widespread Okinawan protests against the American occupation of the islands that followed in the early postwar period. Okinawa was under US military rule and had no independent political autonomy. Yet rather than fight oppression with anger and aggression, the vast majority of Okinawa's postwar political protests, undertaken in the main by the baby-boom generation who had suffered or borne witness to wartime atrocities, were peacefully led by a broadly aligned and mostly left-of-centre populous. *Left* in this sense refers to what was essentially a pro-wealth redistribution, anti-American sentiment, triggered in response to poor living conditions under US occupation. This led to many of those who were politically active on Okinawa sympathizing with or joining the global Marxist-derived movements of communist or socialist states, such as the Soviet Union and later Mao's China. Ultimately, this allowed the Japan Communist Party (JCP) to gain a firm foothold in the prefecture, but initially it combined both pro-reversion to Japanese rule leftists and pro-Okinawan independence groups.

Much of this cohort, despite having inherited a deep-rooted suspicion of mainland Japanese, many of whom colonized their grandparents and discriminated against their parents, nevertheless identified the occupying American forces and their servicemembers as the primary political enemy. After all, it was the Americans they were being occupied by, in contrast to the GoJ who largely supported the reversion of Okinawa to Japanese rule. Okinawans thereby mostly regarded reunification with Japan (rather than independence from Tokyo) as their most attractive and attainable route to emancipation and equality (Mason 2016). This political disposition was not only due to the horrific military bombardment suffered during the Battle of Okinawa but also as a response to the egregious crimes and double standards witnessed in its aftermath at the hands of US forces. These included widespread physical, sexual and economic abuse of the local population. As time went on, these unwanted aspects of postwar Okinawan life became associated increasingly – and quite deliberately by more extreme left-leaning forces – with an unequal capitalistic American system. Constrained under such a system, as opportunist political actors saw and projected it, Okinawa was being oppressed by a domineering foreign superpower (Okinawa Times 2015).

Conversely, a small number of landowners and local business actors with powerful vested interests in relevant industries, such as real estate, construction and concrete, as discussed in greater depth in Chapter 3, benefitted disproportionately from an infusion of hard American dollars. This was in contrast with the majority of their fellow islanders, who made up a comparatively impoverished Okinawan mass society. This elite class of wealthy Okinawans generally identified with the US capitalist dream of financial prosperity, but rather than seeking wealth redistribution or greater equality among their peers, they sought to protect their socio-economic advantage and political influence. This was achieved by remaining as a limited but influential and loosely affiliated minority. Indeed it was this influence that ultimately led to a political body growing into what became known in the post-reversion era as *hoshuha*, or conservative, as wealth and development grew in the prefecture over time. This is now typically contrasted with the *kakushinha*, or progressive, centre-left position. The former retains the support of an extensive US presence on Okinawa (Sakurazawa 2014).

Conservative here, therefore, refers to what might typically be considered centre-right in a European or North American political context, and such vested interests remain to this day staunchly opposed to what was from the outset seen as the communist threat from states falling first under Soviet, and later Chinese, influence during the ensuing Cold War. Okinawa's conservative elements also now assume broad alignment, and in many Okinawan municipalities direct affiliation, with Japan's long-standing conservative ruling party, the LDP.[3] Meanwhile,

---

3 In addition to there now being two of four Diet members for Okinawa representing the LDP (four of six if including additional proportional representation-determined Diet seats), the party has more elected local municipal assembly members than any other party. The JCP currently holds

particularly during the pre-reversion period of 1945–72, the majority of locals were left well short of the improved living standards that they increasingly witnessed being enjoyed by their mainland Japanese counterparts, as a result of Tokyo's postwar "economic miracle". Tokyo was seen to be benefiting from the full independence it gained through the San Francisco Treaty of 1951, while Okinawa remained constrained by military occupation and a lack of any real political autonomy.

This convergence of circumstances, combining dissatisfaction and perceived victimhood with a sense of being left behind, further empowered the leftist forces within Okinawa. These included both small union and community groups, as well as factions of larger national parties such as the JCP, who offered a counternarrative to US propaganda in the form of freedom and equality spurred on in the context of a global Cold War competition between capitalism and communism. Indeed, initially the latter appeared to be winning. Consequently, in an environment where – despite a formal alliance with the US – Japan's political future was still finely balanced between the ideological left and right (or Soviet camp versus US camp), these political actors became overwhelmingly both anti-American and pro-reversion (to Japan). In pursuit of these two prongs of ideologically based politics, the collective convergent left hoped to revert Okinawa to Japanese rule in an era when it was still considered a credible possibility that a non-aligned socialist, or at least centre-left (but still increasingly rich and prosperous), Japanese state might become a reality of which Okinawa could become a part (Stockwin 1962: 33). This ultimately meant giving up on, or at least making a leap of faith with regard to, Okinawan independence. Those who harked back to the eras of the Ryukyus in fighting for outright independence were subsumed within the reversion movement. Those who remained loyal to dreams of creating a modern Ryukyu state under a

---

one of the four Diet seats. It should also be noted that the LDP, despite its name, is neither liberal nor very democratic (or in fact operating as one unified party), with power being contested between powerful intra-party factions or *ha*, which are typically associated with powerful industrial interests and their large conglomerates, or *zaibatsu*. The link between money and politics is a nationwide issue in Japan, but given the unique historical circumstances of Okinawa outlined above, it is unsurprisingly of particular controversy in terms of governing the Islands.

unique ethos thereafter became a tiny minority, as they remain today (Ryukyu Shimpo 2023b).

The realization of reversion to Japanese rule in 1972 ushered in a new structure of domestic politics on Okinawa. The islands once again became a fully assimilated prefecture of Japan (see Figure 2.1). Unfortunately, for those who were seeking to become part of a socialist Japan, Tokyo's conservative LDP-led government ultimately aligned firmly with the US within the Cold War divide. This meant that there was a major cleavage created between national and local politics, but despite local authorities formally being empowered with a degree of autonomy under Article 95 of Japan's postwar constitution, in reality Okinawa, as with other prefectures, was at the behest of legislators and their backers in Tokyo. Nevertheless, the legacy of this political climate on Okinawa was a politically active generation that, even after reversion to Japanese rule, was staunchly opposed to US bases on Okinawa's islands.

The progressives also countered the conservative forces of Japan's ruling LDP party that aligned so closely with successive American administrations (Hashimoto 2019; see also Tasevski 2022). This opposition was partly a legacy of the angry protests that occurred throughout the years leading up to Okinawa's reversion, as part of what was in collective opposition to US land grabs and individual crimes termed the *shimagurumi tōsō*, or island-wide struggles. These peaked during the Koza riots of 1971, in which American-owned cars were overturned and burned in the streets of what is now Okinawa City, then Koza, adjacent to some of the US's largest military facilities on the island. Though only a relatively minor element when compared to underlying economic interests driving the reversion process (see Chapter 3 for further discussion), those who backed the protests believed that it was this kind of grassroots opposition to US rule that ultimately facilitated Okinawa's return to Japan.

In contrast, as living standards improved and poverty decreased in the years that followed reversion, political apathy increased. Moreover, despite sporadic outbursts of anger in response to specific incidents and accidents, concerted political action in opposition waned. What remained was mostly as a function of the US's ongoing use of Okinawan bases from which to launch military campaigns into Southeast Asia, such as during the Vietnam War, so the ending of the Cold War dealt a hammer blow to the collective left in terms of undermining their socialist-informed ideology. More concretely, those who identified as not simply opposing the US military bases but also fighting against the broader impositions of American imperialism and market capitalist ideology found that the credibility of a socialist alternative was jeopardized as a function of failed communist projects in the Soviet Union, China and elsewhere.

As a result, from the 1990s onwards, the ideological strength and militant power of the by then mostly ageing leftist political actors on Okinawa began to lose traction and political support. This included a decline in membership and popularity of sympathetic parties such as the Social Democratic Party and Japan Liberal Party, as well as reduced influence for the JCP itself. In their place, a more neoliberal generation of centre-right politicians and citizens groups, often closely affiliated with the ruling LDP, emerged to fill the political vacuum and cement Okinawa's position in political terms as accruing no greater autonomy than any other prefecture of Japan. These political forces, led by local offices of the LDP, reinforced the conservative vis-à-vis progressive dichotomy as the two established pillars of post-Cold War Okinawan mainstream political identity.

Within this, the division did not by any means eliminate opposition to the scale and form of American basing, as local politicians still had to cater to a populous that remained generally in favour of reducing the oversized footprint of US facilities clogging Okinawa Main Island. However, in reflection of Japanese national politics, local authorities across the prefecture began to project the idea that Okinawa's deteriorating regional security environment required strong political support for a robust US–Japan alliance. This also included overseeing a shifting of the ideational goalposts to a position where neoliberal free-market economic models became assumed as the norm, rather than contested by conservative and progressive factions. Concomitantly, the progressive side moved its focus from seeking equality and a reduction in the burden of US military bases shouldered by Okinawa to that of commercial development and increased relative prosperity.

This meant greater alignment with traditionally conservative elements, such as big business and central government, in various sectors. These included: concrete, construction, tourism and, to an extent, even security (Jiji Press News 2022). Those identified as politically moderate progressives thereby became broadly aligned with the interests of the industry sector-based business elites who dominate these key industries, as identified above. Furthermore, despite popular support for a small number of vocal prefectural governors who have opposed further US military base construction and supported the reduction of bases, such as Masahide Ota, Takeshi Onaga and Denny Tamaki, the more activist elements of the self-identified progressive wing of politics on Okinawa are now largely limited to scholarly academic opposition, the dissemination of protest narratives and small-scale sit-in protests at various US (and increasingly JSDF) military facilities around the prefecture. Even in these cases, many leading figures, including former Governor Takeshi Onaga, with supposedly progressive identities have either historically or while in office been affiliated to Japan's ruling LDP-led conservative coalition. In that regard, this seemingly contradictory double affiliation and dual political identity evidently limits their ability to credibly galvanize broad-based opposition against central government policies. To circumvent this contradiction, such actors have, instead, tended to invest political capital in evoking Okinawa as a historical identity that focuses attention on single issues, such as the new military base being built on top of Henoko Bay. Due to the controversial and complex nature of such issues, however, this approach tends to stimulate further division and conflict.[4]

Among the general population, meanwhile, the status and welfare of the nuclear family and the success of individuals measured in socio-economic terms have largely come to take precedence over grand political ideologies and shared causes (Watanabe 2012). The evidence for this trend having infiltrated the domain of mainstream politics on Okinawa includes representation among the legislature, as in the past ten years Okinawa's handful of National Diet seats have increasingly been won in general elections by the LDP, who broadly support this

4 Okinawa Prefecture justifies its formal position on this in a statement on its official website, entitled "Okinawaken ga futenma hikōjo no henoko isetsu ni hantai suru riyū" [The reasons why Okinawa Prefecture opposes the relocation of Futenma Airbase to Henoko], 5 October 2022, https://www.pref.okinawa.jp/heiwakichi/futenma/1017409/1017413.html.

neoliberalization of societal structures. At the same time, partly as a by-product spawned from the social inequality that this shift towards individualist consumerism has caused, the political climate remains in flux.[5] More specifically, the US-led world order is now perceived to be in crisis and liberal capitalist economies more generally are being seen as unable to provide an environment where (middle-class) citizens can thrive. Such a socio-political milieu creates uncertainty across the country, including on Okinawa. This often comes in the form of rural depopulation, urbanization and desperate attempts by local and central authorities to reverse these trends through incentivizing deurbanization (Chiavacci 2022). By contrast, demographically, Okinawa bucks the national trend with steady growth and a somewhat more distributed population, but incomes remain low and dissatisfaction with the administration in Tokyo continues to grow.

This political turbulence, however, has not seen conservative elements lose power in place of a renewed socialism or pacifism. Quite the reverse. Rather, it seems disillusionment with politicians' perceived inability to bring about higher living standards or greater security appears to have pushed Okinawa, along with the rest of Japanese society, in a more nationalistic direction. There are several indicators that evidence this trend. For example, as indicated by opinion poll data, although a majority of contemporary Okinawans would like to see the number and scope of US bases on the islands reduced, they are also in favour of strengthening the US–Japan alliance and identify the expansion of China as a serious threat that requires substantial investment in order to counter it.[6] Moreover, the animosity shown towards American basing and related activities is substantially greater than that directed against the increase in JSDF stationing across Okinawa. Indeed, despite still being contested, for the most part the latter is tacitly supported or accepted as essential.

5 This phenomenon has become even further exacerbated by economic pressures resulting from governmental responses to the Covid-19 pandemic and war in Ukraine.

6 Japan's Cabinet Office provides specific polling data, including on the issue of US bases and JSDF forces under the title "Naikakufu yoron chōsa: beigunkichi/jieitai" [Cabinet opinion poll: American military bases and the Self Defense Forces], https://survey.gov-online.go.jp/r04/r04-bouei/gairyaku.pdf.

In addition, amid this shift towards support for a more robust Japanese military capability throughout the islands, those further to the political right garner support through the inflation or evocation of the supposed threat posed by a rising and expansionist China, against which Okinawa is at the tip of Japan's analogous defensive spear (see Handa 2023). Therefore, in spite of continued prefecture-wide popular opposition to American bases, the wider political transition in terms of backing increased fortifications also includes seemingly contradictory local support for a strong US–Japan security alliance. Correspondingly, within this trend, a more robustly independent "middle-power" identity is attached to Japan. Once again, these changes come with no small degree of irony given both the history of Okinawa detailed above and the creation of further potential targets along the archipelago for would-be adversaries by contemporary US and GoJ conservatives. Yet greater interoperability with American forces and fortification of Okinawan islands is largely accepted as being essential because of what is depicted by nationalistic government authorities and mainstream media as an increasingly harsh security environment.

GEOGRAPHICAL AND GENERATIONAL DIVISIONS

Though by no means entirely uniform across each societal subgroup, the geographical and social divisions outlined above are an endemic constraint upon any form of Okinawan unity that might be galvanized into a meaningful political force. This includes movements directed by recent prefectural administrations under the slogan of "all Okinawa". The phrase itself is little more than a rhetorical gimmick employed primarily by local politicians, such as the former governors named above, to oppose construction of the new US military base – approved by the GoJ as the replacement facility for MCAS Futenma – atop the coral reef submerged beneath Okinawa's northern Henoko and Oura bays. However, its broader symbolic significance is considerable in terms of binding together stakeholders from islands scattered hundreds of miles apart with greatly differing histories under a single Ryukyuan identity.[7]

7 This is explained and promoted by the Ōruokinawa kaigi (All Okinawa group).

Conversely, partly as a result of both internal migration within Okinawa Prefecture and the kinds of generational changes already documented in this chapter, conflicting identities adopted among different sections of Okinawan society weaken the ability of Okinawans to concentrate action and agency in a concerted form. This includes centralized attempts by the Prefectural Government and applies, for example, to initiatives to revive and promote historical ideals of pacifism and regionalism. The evocation of these tropes might otherwise contribute more substantively towards reducing the upwardly calibrated threat perceptions being disseminated by central government and Japan's mainstream conservative media in relation to Okinawa's vulnerability writ large. As it is, partly as a function of their limited catch-all appeal, most single-issue campaigns emanating from Okinawa are yet to have a significant long-term impact in terms of averting the escalation in tensions surrounding the islands witnessed in recent years.[8]

The issues here are further complicated by specific localized discrepancies within Okinawa Prefecture. For example, this is particularly acute in terms of vastly differing wartime and postwar experiences between the different Okinawan islands. The result has been what is often termed as *ondosa*, or difference of temperature, not only between Okinawans and mainland Japanese but also in terms of the political dispositions that dominate thinking among the various populations of small and medium-sized off-islands. Okinawa Main Island residents, for instance, tend to have a more anti-base stance than their off-island counterparts. This is because of the overwhelming majority of American military facilities being concentrated on the main island and the negative impacts these unsolicited installations have brought about since their construction in the aftermath of the Pacific War. Side-effects include crime, pollution and congestion (Hook, Mason & O'Shea 2015). Moreover, although the bases were built after hostilities had ceased, the Battle of Okinawa itself was termed the Americans' "typhoon of

8 Okinawa Prefecture has promoted this vision of Okinawa through public events, such as the 1 May 2023 "Okinawaken shusai shinpojiumu 'kōryū – taiwa de tsukuru ajia taiheiyō chiiki no heiwa to mirai'" [Okinawa Prefectural Government hosted symposium "Creating a peaceful future for the Asia-Pacific region through exchange and dialogue"].

steel" by director John Junkerman in depicting the relentless bombardment of the main island during the Allied onslaught at the end of Japan's failed Second World War campaign (Junkerman 2016a). The massive ship-to-land shelling operation deliberately targeted Okinawa's administrative and operational core, including surrounding outposts such as the tiny Kerama Islands and Ie-jima Island. In contrast, some of the larger off-islands, such as Ishigaki Island, saw relatively very little bloodshed as a direct result of armed combat during the conflict. As we shall see in later chapters, in a reversal of this stark disparity during wartime, Ishigaki Island and the Yaeyama Islands cluster that it sits within now have a more front-line position in potential confrontations with adversaries such as China, which once again illustrates the gap between different Okinawan islands. Nevertheless, this only serves to underline how differing experiences in relation to changing events or circumstances give rise to distinct political dispositions that are a further source of friction, resentment or contestation.

At the same time, counter-intuitively, there are multiple specific locales on the main island immediately adjacent to bases that are actually in favour of their continued presence, and even expansion. This is because of the direct economic benefits that American military facilities offer through contributions to land taxes, tourism and consumption. Henoko Village, situated next-door to the controversial new base construction site as an extension of the US Marine Corps' Camp Schwab, which is opposed by over 70 per cent of the Okinawan population as a whole, is a case in point (Williams 2013). There, in a reversal of the prefecture-wide referendum result, more than the same proportional majority of Henoko Villagers support construction of the new base facility. On the other hand, for those residing on major off-islands, such as the larger Yaeyama Islands (including Ishigaki Island and Yonaguni Island) and Miyakojima Island, the debate around the expanded stationing of JSDF, rather than American, military facilities is of greatest concern. It also generates similarly divisive narrative debates over costs and benefits.[9] Additionally, it is, of course, worth noting that because of the hierarchical political structure mapped out at the start (see Figure 2.1), the will of the people, as represented by referendums or opinion polls, is

9 The broader impact of these changes is discussed in Asahi Digital (2023).

rarely reflected meaningfully within the governance process that administers these sites. Rather, decisions are taken and enforced by ruling LDP ministers and their bureaucratic officials in Tokyo, who in effect assume a powerful mandate provided for them at the national level because of weak and divided opposition within the National Diet.

Amid this context, the overall positive impact of American (and JSDF) bases on Okinawa is often greatly exaggerated by partial central government authorities and commercial vested interests, not to mention the US Department of State, as well as both countries' military forces and mainstream media (see Mainichi Shimbun 2022). The extent of the exaggeration is particularly evident when one considers the physical land space that they occupy. Military facilities take up almost 20 per cent of Okinawa Main Island's total land area and more than 30 per cent of Ie-Jima Island. When returned, these land areas can be used productively for other purposes, such as science, tourism and alternative commercial activities.[10] Nevertheless, as discussed in greater depth in Chapter 3, even when land is returned, it is not always used to the maximum benefit of Okinawans. What is more, the picture is further complicated by the fact that some small and relatively depopulated settlements, such as Henoko Village noted above, have become socio-economically base-reliant, leading to a political milieu that reflects such reliance in its support for the status quo or additional base-related development, construction and diversification.

Nevertheless, the dangers of hosting bases remain clear. For example, MCAS Futenma, in the middle of densely populated Ginowan City, is particularly dangerous and breaches the US's own laws ensuring an extended clearance zone around military facilities. Furthermore, the above-mentioned Henoko Village for instance, which is far more isolated, has come to rely almost entirely upon base-related income to sustain its economy, which in itself constrains the capacity of a more broad-based local economy to flourish (Rabson 2012). If both US and Japanese militaries are combined, these kinds of specific base-dependent areas include the key off-islands already identified along the First Island

10 The Japan MOD's 2017 white paper discusses reclaimed land usage, "Susumu okinawa no tochi henkan to atochi riyō" [Advancements in the return of Okinawan land and its usages (editorial)].

Chain, incorporating Ighisgaki Island, Miyakojima Island and particularly Yonaguni Island. Here, as otherwise depopulating local authorities, they have recently approved and opened new JSDF facilities within their jurisdictions under the auspices of helping to encourage more youthful in-migration and boost growth, as well as strengthen security. After all, the political tide is already largely in favour of further JSDF bases and fortification to protect against the perceived or constructed threats posed by China and Taiwan-related contingencies, as well as acting as a boon for short-term economic investment and spin-off industries on these islands. The framing of threat narratives, however, drives a wedge between those seeking to promote more cordial exchange-based relations with Asian states, such as Taiwan and mainland China, and those happy to alienate them, particularly the latter, in the name of facing down expansionism, authoritarianism and ultimately would-be military aggression.[11]

In the case of constructing new JSDF facilities and the deployment of their servicemembers into rural island areas, the presence of relatively young personnel and their families is thereby promoted as a means by which to prevent further ageing and depopulation of these remote outposts and rejuvenate growth. This dynamic, therefore, tends to tip the balance of political support in favour of such fortifications as a quick fix for the so-called lost decades of sluggish economic growth since Japan's economic bubble burst in 1991. These hit already depopulated remote locales hard and have now been exacerbated by a severe post-financial crisis and post-Covid socio-economic malaise.[12] Facing the relatively urgent need to address these challenges, the potential longer-term dangers of transforming the Okinawa Island chain into a would-be target in any contingency situation are, understandably, masked or deprioritized in the process. Here, the increased risk of being targeted by Chinese missiles or other assailants as a result of deploying state-of-the-art weaponry against them on these islands has not been lost on local residents, but these risks are deemed – albeit often only by a narrow majority – to be outweighed by the greater perceived benefits.[13]

11 The dynamics surrounding this issue are discussed in Panda (2023).

12 For documentation of Yonaguni's demographic decline, see Jiji Press (2022).

13 For opinion polling data that detail this contestation, see *Ryukyu Shimpo* (2023b).

Further, the potentially positive impact that new resident military personnel may have on younger generations is prioritized on demographic grounds in terms of sustaining the local society and political economy. Simply put, citizens of working age largely no longer wish to rely on, or politically support, the kinds of labour-intensive primary industries, such as fishing and sugar cane farming, that their parents and grandparents undertook for a living. Hence, without younger people being stationed on these islands, those of productive age will leave rural settlements to their rapidly ageing populations and seek opportunities in urban areas, both within and outside of the prefecture. However, such migration does little to alleviate the underlying causes of a growing division between intergenerational Okinawan identities and may actually exacerbate the broader issues of political polarization across Okinawa as a whole. Furthermore, there is endemic apathy among Okinawa's youth, including those of productive working age, towards the preservation or continuation of a distinctly pacifist historical Okinawan identity. This phenomenon is particularly acute when it comes to the active representation of such an identity within the political process. As one working-aged resident of Itoman City put it, "if Okinawa is so great as it is, why try to change it?"[14] The result is that, even if not proactive supporters of the ruling LDP, the population is increasingly aligned with, or at least not actively opposed to, a governmental position that points towards confronting regional adversaries with military power as a continuation of politics by other means, which may envelope these vulnerable islands.

On the other side of this generational divide, residents old enough to remember being shelled by Allied ships during the Battle of Okinawa are particularly sensitive to the prospect of stationing what are undoubtedly potential targets for a prospective "coming war with China" (Pilger 2017). For example, the new JSDF facility on Miyakojima Island was built to house missiles with a defensive remit, but in the future could be the subject of something equivalent to mission creep that leads towards hosting a counter-strike capability of combined US–Japan forces explicitly designed for targeting Chinese strike capabilities aimed at the First Island Chain. The base is fewer than 500 metres from the nearest

14 Interview with Itoman City resident, 9 April 2024.

inhabited village. This is a settlement housing mainly elderly residents who vehemently opposed the base's construction at the local level but were outvoted and outmuscled by the municipality as a whole, including the incumbent Mayor Zakimi, backed by powerful central government actors and officials (see Burke & Koja 2022). Meanwhile, younger residents cite the need for this and two other substantial JSDF facilities on the island as a means by which to protect the 50,000 strong community. Where, as one islander pointed out, they used to look out for whales from across their geographically vulnerable and exposed coastline, it is now more gripping to try and spot Chinese aircraft carriers and submarines as they penetrate the straits either side of Miyakojima Island on their way to and from the East China Sea into the open Pacific Ocean.[15]

OCCUPATIONAL HAZARDS, EXPLOITATION AND INCENTIVES

Considering the clear disparities and domestic friction points discussed thus far, it might be assumed that Okinawa could be effectively examined if viewed through the lens of class struggle. Instead, it is often crudely framed only in a binary historical contrast between Okinawans and mainland Japanese in terms of the persecution and discrimination of the former by the ruling class of the latter (Matsumura 2015). If addressed with greater nuance, however, class divisions between different occupational groups and industries have been, and remain, a significant element of political contestation on Okinawa. This includes in relation to both base politics and post-reversion Japanese rule, neither of which can be easily overstated. After all, the postwar struggle for reversion to mainland Japanese rule was itself as much a battle to secure greater investment from, and integration into, the booming Japanese economy – with all of its wealthy industrial sectors – than it was to improve democracy and human rights (Hoshino 2013). Amid what transpired, evidence of socio-economic exploitation, perversely incentivized competition and occupational hierarchy is everywhere. A curious mixture

15 The observation was gleaned from an interview with a prospective Miyakojima mayoral candidate, 13 April 2023.

of these aspects quite literally shapes the fabric of not only society but also the very land of Okinawa itself. As discussed further in Chapter 3, one only has to observe the unnaturally rectangular shape of the main island's reclaimed southwest coastline, for example, to see the extent to which relentless concrete and gravel-based construction in the name of industrial development is paramount in this regard (see Figure 2.2).

The prioritization of such industries by a dominant business class that is in alignment with the ruling political establishment, thereby, has

Figure 2.2 Okinawa's disfigured central and southwest coast following the development of multiple land reclamation projects

Source: iStock.

serious consequences for the majority of those who are less privileged. Not least, they are essentially forced to accept a hyper-industrialized view of progress and prosperity. The effects are chaotic. For instance, while road construction may ease transport links in some areas of the islands, the mass building of coastal tourist resorts, mostly by large mainland companies, has effectively excluded locals who cannot afford to use them from using their own coasts. It has also changed natural coastlines beyond all recognition. Meanwhile, the building of new military bases, as well as the presence of existing defence facilities, is a serious cause of travel congestion, because of the extensive land space they take up throughout the middle of Okinawa Main Island. US facilities also have their own coastal strips for training and recreation that exclude Okinawan residents who do not hold American passports or base permits. As a self-reinforcing feedback loop, this land usage issue feeds into the justification for promoting further construction-based projects to alleviate the congested areas, allowing new roads, ports and monorail extensions to be constructed in order to mitigate against the associated issues of overcrowding. The irony is that these problems were themselves largely a result of industrial expansion manifest in infrastructure that has, arguably, done little to meaningfully benefit most Okinawans. What is less often fully documented is that the income from such infrastructure projects overwhelmingly finds its way into the pockets of large mainland companies, with minimal profits being distributed to local enterprises and Okinawan workers (see Fisher 2017).

In this regard, as argued convincingly by avid Ryukyu nationalist and Ryukoku University professor Yasukatsu Matsushima, powerful mainland Japanese companies and corporations sustain what he has described as neocolonial type relationships. These have been facilitated by reversion to Japanese rule, because there are no longer any tariffs applied to transactions between Okinawa and mainland Japan. Pre-reversion, these were paid by Japanese enterprises that wanted access to the – albeit US-controlled – Okinawan market. After reverting to standard Japanese prefectural status, this meant that numerous small and medium-sized companies based on Okinawa were unable to compete with larger Japanese corporations that suddenly entered into their market with all the legal changes and tariff barrier removals that were enacted at the time of reversion in 1972.[16] In that sense, despite prefecture-wide special tax-breaks and government funding schemes, Okinawan commercial enterprises still have a limited ability to gain an advantage within their own prefecture. This makes the development of a Ryukyu Kingdom-style political economy in which the leaders of local trade and commerce might independently develop a stable, self-sufficient network of business relationships with surrounding states and economic actors difficult to realize.

This kind of occupational class structure on Okinawa is also relevant as a source of conflict in areas where there is competition between multiple industries over use of the same physical space. For instance, the push to secure contracts and government budgets for construction-based infrastructural development is often – unsuccessfully – countered by those who would benefit more from cleaner fishing waters, a less built up and more natural coastline aimed at increased ecotourism, and broader-based environmental preservation. In this sense, although there is no clearly delineated hierarchy in terms of specific occupations and industries explicitly linked to predesignated classes, there are clearly winners and losers that are defined mostly by the specific divisions between Japan's mainland and Okinawa-based actors, as well as by sectors intersecting a range of specializations (Shimada 2018). In cases where big business – particularly the three "Ks" of *kankō* (tourism), *kensetsu* (construction) and *kichi* (bases) – dominates or pushes out competing interests, the losers are (usually with good reason) resentful of the winners, which causes a knock-on effect into the political sphere. Concretely, it often forces indigenous small-scale industries with ageing workforces, such as pottery, fishing and limited agricultures, out of business or into greatly reduced production. Those connected to such sectors then galvanize around anti-base and anti-LDP sentiment, but their political power is waning over time. The victims of these changes and

16 This process of market penetration and domination by giant Japanese corporations, many with close links to government as part of Japan's so-called "iron triangle" (ruling party, bureaucracy and big business) that sustain a form of neo-colonialism has been detailed by Matsushima Yasukatsu and others at the UN, as explained to the author in an interview with Matsushima on 16 May 2023 at Ryukoku University, Kyoto.

their resulting economic disparity thereby serve as further evidence of the continuation of discrimination by mainland Japanese elites backed by US forces operating in de facto unison vis-à-vis Okinawan islanders.

In another instance of this interest-based political competition, Okinawa's local fishermen, many of whom have become disenfranchised and relatively poorer in recent decades, and environmental activists working on and around the islands' fragile marine ecospheres have in some cases joined forces. Therein, they not only bemoan the increasingly polluted and reclaimed coastal waters but actively fight using small boats to obstruct base projects and land reclamation through physical demonstrations and sabotage of construction sites. Indeed, these activities often act as catalysts or focal points for disputes between central and local government authorities, such as in the case of the new base under construction at Henoko.[17] They therefore also contribute indirectly towards increasing tensions between the GoJ and the US. This is because the latter attempts to outsource all *domestic* issues to its junior alliance partner (here the national government authorities of Japan) as the preferred means by which to supress dissent and at the same time demand specific kinds of facilities be built and supplied for American forces to use under the remit of the US–Japan Security Alliance. Hence, pushback from local protestors towards GoJ policies implemented under the pretext of upholding the alliance leads to higher-profile figures from Tokyo's political elite having to take up these issues with their counterparts in Washington. Fractures in this three-layer – US, Japan, Okinawa – relationship thereby add to the complexities that face policy-making across the region. This includes managing political divisions, avoiding economic disruption and mitigating real or perceived weakness within the alliance.

Of course, in many commercial areas, such as transport, tourism and scientific projects, powerful political interests generally align more than they compete. However, even here the structure and form of development relies in some cases on increasing wealth disparity among the local population, the marginalization of culturally significant sectors – such as the dwindling but traditionally central fishing

17 At the construction site offshore of Henoko, the dispute also involves international NGOs; see Greenpeace (2016).

industry – and an influx of tourists who, although welcome as a source of revenue, frequently create environmental and cultural concerns or hazards. For instance, mainland Chinese tourists have been accused by local tradespeople of rudeness, littering and other culturally challenging behaviour, meaning that the income they are providing through consumption within the local economy does little to improve the image of, or deepen ties with, Okinawa as their historical suzerain.[18] Simply put, more tourists on Okinawa does not always mean a reduction in tensions. Furthermore, the link between reliance upon their economic income and integration, on the one hand, and adverse political influence upon Japan's domestic processes of (nominally) democratic governance, on the other, has been claimed by nationalist factions at both local and national levels. This creates further points of conflict on the islands. At the same time, more generally, residents and political leaders struggle to reconcile the seemingly contradictory objectives of increasing tourism from mainland Asia and elsewhere to bolster growth in the economy, while simultaneously protecting the First Island Chain from a rapidly expanding regional hegemonic power in the form of Xi Jinping's China.

OKINAWAN INTERESTS VERSUS NATIONAL POLITICAL INTEREST

One of the primary reasons for fearing that Okinawa will become a flashpoint amid the contested domestic interests and increasing regional influence of China identified above is the response of Japan's national governmental authorities to the unfolding situation. Perhaps of greatest concern is the lack of compelling evidence to suggest that the current LDP administration, with its dominant mandate under protracted one-party rule, is doing anything other than continuing a de facto policy of treating Okinawa as a tool of national defence, or the previously termed *suteishi*, in its protection of the First Island Chain.[19]

18 This was confirmed with Okinawa-based small business owners and other entrepreneurs regarding the behaviour of particular nationalities of tourists in a series of in-person interviews conducted between 14 and 17 April 2023.

19 For confirmation of this process, see Hiroshima Media Centre (2015).

There is widespread popular and party political opposition to the use of disproportionately extensive American basing on Okinawa for this purpose, but in alignment, and to varying degrees complicity, with the mainstream national media the GoJ appears to have been successful in persuading a majority of mainland citizens that this usage and increased fortification of Okinawa with JSDF facilities is the "only option" to ensure national security.[20] This framing is particularly prevalent in the national NHK television and conservative newspaper press coverage, which continues to present Okinawans as victims of geography, circumstances and bad luck, but does little to compensate these elements or emancipate them from their historically rooted position of colonial subjugation (see Asahi Shimbun 2023a).

As noted at the outset, Okinawa has been dominated by two, or arguably three, colonial powers stemming from its roots as a tributary state of China, through colonization by Japan, occupation by the US and finally return to Japanese rule as a prefectural authority. In this respect, as already noted, the legacy of historical Ryukyuan independence, political subjugation and struggles for greater autonomy, in combination, cast a long shadow over the relationship between the prefecture and the central GoJ. Here too, though, the generational and spatial changes identified above matter. Younger generations are, according to qualitative research and opinion poll data,[21] more invested in Japan as their primary identity than their parents and grandparents were, although both are broadly in favour of a reduction in military bases (see Table 2.1). In that sense, although seeking reversion for socio-economic and political reasons, older generations are, unlike their next generation, inclined to view the GoJ as essentially an oppressor of Okinawan political self-determination rather than the facilitator of Okinawan voices or guarantor of its peace and security. This tendency is also evidenced by the increased number of parliamentary seats now held by ruling LDP candidates and a waning of support for those who vehemently oppose national policies that iden-

20 Based on multiple opinion polls conducted by the Japanese Cabinet Office; the disparity of opinion is reflected across press outlets, as detailed in Asahi Shimbun (2022).

21 For further discussion, see relevant cabinet and newspaper opinion polls, as well as academic scholarship on Okinawan identity (see "Guide to further reading").

Table 2.1 Opinion poll data on key issues for Okinawan residents

Questions	*Responses*				
In view of Okinawa's reversion to Japanese rule, the status of bases is a problem. What do you think should be done about bases on Okinawa?	Bases should be retained as they are (5.4%)	Bases should be used freely except for nuclear weapons (8.5%)	Bases on Okinawa should be made equivalent to those on the mainland (45.9%)	All bases should be removed (17.4%)	Unsure / Don't know (22.7%)
Do you agree with the opinion that "base land should be returned ASAP"?	Agree (79.6%)	Disagree (1.8%)	Cannot generalize (10.9%)	–	(7.7%)
Concerning the issue of timing, when do you think the land occupied by bases should be returned?	Within 2–3 years (59.6%)	Within 4–5 years (7.8%)	After more than 5 years (1.5%)	–	(31.1%)
Are bases on Okinawa currently helping to ensure the peace and security of Japan and East Asia?	Yes, greatly (13.6%)	Somewhat (33.9%)	They are not (22.2%)	–	(30.4%)

Source: Compiled by the author from Cabinet Office and national newspaper opinion polls.

tify the need to further fortify the Ryukyu Islands and intensify their use by the JSDF. The same trend applies to popular support for integrating US and Japanese military forces. At the same time, with the relatively powerful immediate postwar pro-Okinawan independence movement having been subsumed within the push for reversion – and now reduced to little more than a small gathering of like-minded students and academics – there is limited scope for any kind of grassroots political movement to challenge national narratives. This includes opposition to the projection and dissemination of those that put Okinawa at the front and centre of preparations for conflict with China (Mason 2019; see also Kelly 2022).

In this sense, as national media narratives backed by a mostly central government-determined education system permeate youth culture and wider society, conservatism is growing on Okinawa. For example, elementary and junior high schools must adopt the entirety of the national curriculum and are explicitly forbidden from teaching a more progressive version of Okinawan history and identity. Indeed, in cases such as on Taketomi Island, where a less nationalistic textbook than had been supplied by central authorities was introduced into the classroom, Japan's Ministry for Education, in an unprecedented move, overrode the normal chain of administrative command (going above the heads of the Okinawa Prefectural Government) in ordering the local authority to restore the original text (see Ryukyu Shimpo 2014). In this way, despite the huge divergence of Ryukyuan history from much of that documented on mainland Japan, very little of these localized differences are taught to the islands' current youth population. In that respect, Japanese nationalist conservatism permeating Okinawan education can be seen as a form of centralized cultural imposition. This trend, which incorporates a broadly pro-US–Japan alliance worldview, is politically right of centre in its leanings, which leads to its broad, if often only implicit, alignment with the LDP. That said, in some cases such standpoints are explicitly backed by the ruling party through support for nationalistic political candidates running in elections at local and national levels.

A further complicating variable, however, is that some prominent Okinawan conservatives do still, nonetheless, in the main seek a greater degree of self-autonomy and recognition for Okinawa than is currently at their command. In other words, while support for the LDP-backed push towards a more robust US–Japan Security Alliance and firm stance towards China, in combination with a reduction of Okinawa's base burden, may seem contradictory, this is not necessarily how it is perceived from within the prefecture.[22] Conversely, despite advocating a greater degree of autonomy, a majority of younger generation Okinawans, who

22 See Okinawan LDP Diet member statements on national security. Kokkai kaigiroku kensaku shisutemu [National Diet speaker records search system], National Diet Library, Japan, https://kokkai.ndl.go.jp/#/.

mostly identify as Japanese first and Okinawan second (although as a hybrid of the two), see base construction and military interoperability between the US and Japan as necessary to counter a growing challenge posed by Beijing. At the same time, they also identify these as elements that act as the foundation through which contemporary Okinawa can be conserved as a meaningful entity, albeit as a full prefecture of Japan rather than an independent state. Put simply, the political logic here is that only a militarily fortified Okinawa can provide the kinds of security guarantees needed to consolidate a platform from which to develop commercially and culturally based activities that promote Okinawa's unique characteristics and identity.

In that regard, the broader context of Okinawa's divided politics needs to be reconsidered in distinction from Japan's other 46 prefectures if we are to properly understand why there is such potential for the islands' tiny, scattered landmass to become a flashpoint between the great powers. In light of the historical changes to sovereign control (from independence to Japanese, then American, rule and back again), prefecture-specific laws and additional layers of central bureaucracy already discussed, it would be easy to assume that Okinawa is essentially an oppressed polity, overwhelmingly fighting the vice-like grip of central government. In fact, the Prefectural Government's relationship to the ruling LDP and other democratically elected members of the Diet is subtle and complex. For example, there are four directly elected permanent Diet seats designated to Okinawa, in addition to two from the Kyushu proportional representation block, of which a total of four are now held by LDP candidates, marking a strong shift in their favour.[23] Yet it has not been uncommon for former LDP members or affiliates to run as independent candidates against current LDP representatives, with mostly very similar manifestos. The incumbent Prefectural Governor Tamaki Denny's two predecessors were both such cases. As with other liberal democracies, local and national representatives also often diverge in opinion, as is the case among Okinawa's 41 widely dispersed local authorities (cities, towns and villages). However, the issue that causes the greatest division, even in an intra-party context, remains

23 All major national political parties field candidates for the National Diet elections held on Okinawa.

that of military bases. This is all the more so amid the current situation of China being portrayed by a hawkish national security establishment as an exponential existential threat. Popular support is shifting away from more pro-Asia progressive politics towards that of anti-China conservatives, albeit with concerns regarding the continued overstationing of bases on the islands.

For its part, the national government and its supporters in the mainstream media make suitably apologetic noises with regard to the extensive burden that Okinawa shoulders in hosting so many bases. Nevertheless, unsurprisingly, such narratives rarely include comprehensive consideration of the extent to which a combination of US and JSDF bases on Okinawa also act as the mostly likely potential target of any external attack. Undeterred by such concerns, the GoJ pursues an agenda based upon politicized framings of China and North Korea as threats, including by backing sympathetic local government candidates throughout Okinawa Prefecture, especially in key municipalities along the First Island Chain. Recent electoral successes of pro-JSDF base mayors in Miyakojima, Ishigaki and Yonaguni pay testament to the efficacy of this approach (see, e.g., Ryukyu Shimpo 2018). Meanwhile, national agencies such as the Ministry of Foreign Affairs (MOFA), Ministry of Defense (MOD) and the Prime Minister's Cabinet continue to repeat the doctrine of the US–Japan alliance being central to securing Japan's national interests, with Okinawa playing an essential and unavoidable role in this endeavour vis-à-vis the perceived threats deemed to be emanating from mainland Asia (Hook, Mason & O'Shea 2015). Furthermore, this confrontational position of the national government with reference to Okinawa is further reinforced by nationalist opposition parties that push for an even harder line than the ruling LDP. These erode more moderate voices within the GoJ and effectively silence those to the centre-left, including the Constitutional Democrat Party as the largest of these. Hardline political voices are led in the Diet by the Nippon Ishin no Kai (Japan Innovation Party), which has given impetus to moving the conceptual goalposts of prioritizing extreme outer island defence further into a mainstream position. In turn, this has effectively created a political climate where the only established nationwide party promoting de-escalation and further engagement with regional states is the (relatively weak and insubstantial) JCP.

DOMESTIC IDENTITY AMID GREAT POWER POLITICS

The local–national dynamics discussed thus far, then, offer little hope of Okinawa avoiding being forced into a precarious position that – in contradistinction from the Ryukyu Islands' traditional societal values of universal peace and friendship – risks the prefecture becoming Japan's point of greatest physical exposure to external aggression. Unfortunately, the current trends of regional international great power politics are even more alarming for Japan's most outlying local authority. As the US and China deepen their global competition, Japan is increasingly locked into the American side of this divide, placing Okinawa at the fault line of where the two superpowers might lock horns along the East China Sea's (ECS) Indo-Pacific rim. However, Okinawa's distinct domestic identity and historical affinity with all the surrounding states that it has held major relationships with may have an important role to play in shifting the dynamic away from the creation of a flashpoint. After all the Southwest Island Chain is viewed and acted upon by both sides of the US–China divide as both a geographical and conceptual maritime great wall designed to contain China (Son & Mason 2013; Mason & Park 2024). Furthermore, the effect of domestic political support on either side of the Pacific Ocean, not to mention that already discussed on Okinawa itself, for massive fortification of this area is destabilizing, escalatory and multidimensional in terms of its impact.

The specific security aspects of these concerns are discussed in greater detail throughout Chapter 4, but here let us consider how the dilemma faced by Okinawa stretches from local issue politics to the global contest for power. In that regard, the islands have already become a conceptual flashpoint in the sense that they are used to stimulate assertive internal and external foreign policy narratives, backed by deadly weaponry on all sides. These place Okinawa in the crosshairs even if they are mostly notional. For example, American ambiguity demonstrated over the specific issue of assigning sovereignty to the Senkaku Islands is designed by Washington to placate Beijing while reassuring Tokyo of its enduring deterrence capability and, perhaps most importantly, credibility (O'Shea 2019). Meanwhile, because of the Senkaku Islands being administered from Ishigaki Island and included within the scope and remit of the US–Japan Security Alliance, China is seeking to unilaterally alter the status quo and demonstrate strength to its domestic populous, as well as regional onlookers seeking to hedge between the two superpowers. These include many of the Association of Southeast Asian Nations (ASEAN) states. In other words, eroding the de facto control Japan has over these historically contested islands through rhetorical devices and grey-zone tactics is as politically significant as hard-power projection over them.[24] This involves Beijing making statements about China's unequivocal possession of these uninhabited rocks, as well as increasing incursions into and around the islets that might – but Chinese leaders mostly hope will not – provoke a kinetic Japanese response.[25] Such tactics are then presented to China's domestic audience as illustrative of China asserting its rightful ownership over sovereign Chinese territory. These kinds of political gamesmanship can, though, be fraught with escalatory dangers, because once the top-down narrative has been spun and disseminated to the wider public, it thereafter itself compels the regime in Beijing to demonstrate its ability to actually back up words with actions, through diplomatic or, if push comes to shove, military means (Mason & Park 2024: 5).

For the most part, Tokyo and Washington ignore or co-opt Okinawan political voices and respond to what are often portrayed as Chinese provocations with the intention of maintaining a credible position of sovereign control for Japan without escalating to the level of interstate conflict (O'Shea 2015). In that regard, the islands of Okinawa are once again treated by the administrations in the US and the People's Republic of China (PRC) as integral but essentially voiceless entities. Out at sea, this is currently achieved by Japan increasing its strengthening and proactive use of the Japan Coast Guard (JCG), which is part of the Japanese National Police Agency rather than JSDF. This means increased budgets and militarization of the JCG are allocated outside of the defence budget, so reduce the controversy of militarizing local areas. In other words, these changes are more politically palatable for domestic audiences if couched within a framing of law enforcement rather than military

24 This issue was discussed among a predominantly academic audience during public lectures given by the author at Ritsumeikan University (25 May 2023) and Sophia University (2 June 2023).

25 The delicate status quo and shifting dynamics are discussed by Honrada (2023).

operations. At the time of writing, the result is temporarily a tense but manageable standoff between JCG vessels and their Chinese counterparts in the surrounding waters.[26] However, this status quo looks unsustainable on several counts. First, while the US refuses to take a formal position on sovereignty itself, Japan's official stance and public rhetoric on total and non-negotiable sovereignty over the Senkaku Islands is as unambiguous as China's. Moreover, the majority of Ishigaki's islanders, including Mayor Nakayma, firmly support this position. In this sense, in order to keep the fragile peace, Chinese and Japanese authorities are effectively talking past each other at the diplomatic level.

This delicate and dynamic politically driven status quo is reflective of the broader regional context within which Okinawa finds itself. The PRC's growing maritime military power relative to that of Japan's is a concern for such an exposed and luminal territory as the Ryukyu Islands chain, with the Okinawan islands running through its spine in partial encirclement of China's eastern seaboard. Concomitantly, Tokyo's recent and, in the post-Second World War era, unprecedented rise in defence spending to over 2 per cent of gross domestic product risks accelerating an already advanced arms race that places Okinawa as the keystone between two vital expanses of contested seascape. Within this competition, China is steadily catching up with the US.[27] Furthermore, spurred by a toxic and divisive international environment in which the US increasingly identifies China as part of a rival camp that includes American-designated aggressors such as Russia, Iran and North Korea, there is seemingly little short-term hope of reducing regional tensions, particularly concerning the wider ECS rim.

This has additionally serious implications for Okinawa, not least because of its proximity to Taiwan. In the case of any, even cursory, Chinese invasion of the breakaway island province, Beijing's authorities would almost certainly need to authorize the capture of Yonaguni Island and probably Okinawa's Yaeyama Islands as a whole, in order to prevent counter-strike capabilities being operationalized. This would also be essential for the leadership in terms of maintaining its domestic

26 This tense standoff situation is as explained by a JCG officer, 13 February 2023, Chatan, Okinawa.

27 The speed and extent of China's military rise is highlighted by Schuman (2023).

political credibility (Rittenhouse-Green & Talmadge 2022). The PLAN would also potentially be given the green light to attack US Airforce assets at Kadena Airbase on Okinawa's main island. As with the infamous MCAS Futenma and most other US facilities on the islands, Kadena is surrounded by major settlements. The base itself is suspected to already have hundreds of the PLA's state-of-the-art rockets precisely locked onto it as a key ground-based asset target. As already noted, the American facilities on Okinawa have not been established with the same level of physical clearance assigned to bases in the US or mainland Japan, meaning that they are only a few metres away from Okinawan schools, hospitals and other key infrastructure. In this respect, great power politics threatens to inflict very real harms upon a largely powerless population, whether they share in its grand objectives or not.

CONCLUSION

The discussion above has established the significance of Okinawa's unusual domestic politics as a key variable in its positionality. Specifically, this is relevant to the likelihood of Okinawa becoming a regional flashpoint, but it is also critical to its potential for averting such a scenario. Having critically examined the tumultuous recent socio-political and geostrategic history of Okinawa in relation to the present challenges it faces in these areas, it is evident that the islands remain precariously positioned amid escalating conflicts of interest. Domestically, generational divides, historically rooted geographical disparities between the prefecture's distantly scattered island communities and the gradual erosion of Okinawa's unique identity all play into this. As a result, Okinawan society is both fractured and increasingly pushed into alignment with Japan's conservative mainstream forces that support fortification of the First Island Chain against China in close alignment with the US. Moreover, the PRC is now viewed by a majority of Okinawans as a growing and existential threat. This is despite deep historical ties that once saw the Ryukyu Kingdom pay tribute to successive Chinese emperors as a tributary state. Correspondingly, such a nationalistic approach disseminated via political and media elites in Tokyo comes at the potential cost of destroying initiatives driven at the level of the Prefectural Government to harmonize regional relations around the ECS rim.

Okinawa's status – and specifically that of the outlying Ishigaki City – as the local authority that administers the Senkaku Islands further complicates these dynamics. This is because Okinawan local politics is embedded within the fundamental disagreement between Tokyo and Beijing over ownership of these uninhabited islets. Hence, when sub-prefectural political discord is coupled with a dangerously polarized international structure within which the US–Japan alliance identifies China as a rival power (discussed further in Chapter 4), Okinawa is placed at an obvious flashpoint between both competing domestic and great power interests. The risks of real kinetic conflict are heightened by high-level political rhetoric that, although designed primarily for domestic audiences, leaves little room for reconciliation and measured diplomacy out of fear of a nationalist backlash.[28] This has reached a point at which the potential for a contingency involving Taiwan, including where some of Okinawa's outlying municipalities become at least temporarily cut off from Naha as well as Tokyo, is also not insubstantial. For Okinawa, this further exacerbates the dangers of localized political dispute and disunity, particularly given that in any invasion scenario Chinese forces would need to effectively lock down an area of maritime space by force that includes some if not all of these outer islands.

There would, however, undoubtedly be a significant cost to any political decision that leads to an escalation across the ECS. In search, therefore, of other lines of investigation towards more constructive responses to the stark socio-political milieu surrounding Okinawa, Chapter 3 examines the economic drivers of the prefecture's current situation. This addresses the complex issues of Okinawa's relative commercial and financial positionality and offers an exposition of potential routes to a more stable and sustainable regional political economy. In addition, it sheds light on the barriers and challenges that look set to keep Japan's most southwesterly territory in a position where this will be difficult to achieve.

28 The US–Japan alliance's readiness for a kinetic contingency is set out in a series of posts for the Yokosuka Council on Asia Pacific Studies (YCAPS) blog and was further covered in their 22 April 2023 online webinar, "A new era of US–Japan amphibious capabilities". For further discussion see: https://www.ycaps.org/ycaps-jicuf-policy-dialogue.

3

Tracing the money trail

This chapter traces the money trail to expose the commercial interests at play in the conflict over Okinawa and its outer off-islands. In so doing, it also addresses the broader issues of complex economics that surround the prefecture's governance and affect its role in regional international relations. This reveals the historical reasons behind the current state and status of US forces on the Ryukyus, as well as the financial incentives provided for both American and JSDF personnel to be stationed on the islands. It also assesses the economically driven aspects of local Okinawan authorities' policy in terms of their relationship with Chinese and Taiwanese counterparts. This includes discussion of Beijing's claims to the Senkaku Islands, which were only asserted in earnest after oil was discovered beneath the surrounding seabed and Okinawa's reversion to Japan had been provisionally agreed during the 1960s. Therein, these elements are contextualized in contrast with China's recent overtures towards the Okinawan Prefectural Government, which hint at their encouragement of Governor Tamaki Denny's efforts to promote a closer relationship with mainland Asia through regionally based socio-economic exchange. Contrastingly, the often conflicting influence of Japan's national government in providing the *omoiyari yosan*, or sympathy budget, to pay for American troops stationed on Okinawa, as well as its massive domestic aid package in the form of special lump sum payments to local government, is further examined. Particular attention is afforded here to the impact that these funding practices and economic pressures have upon regional dynamics.

Ultimately, the chapter argues that money on Okinawa matters. As such, within the overarching thrust of the volume's focus on this specific locality as a probable flashpoint for broader regional conflict, it is contended that a large range of commercial industries and interests must be accounted for. This includes unpacking how financial incentives and penalties are often in competition with one another, as well as grappling with potential areas of greater synergy. More concretely, by arguing from a decentred Okinawan perspective, the discussion illuminates how further efforts are needed to reduce Okinawa's vulnerability and increase resilience through specialization and diversification. These aspects, particularly in terms of the roles of local businesses and new initiatives, are emphasized as a means by which to ensure more sustainable economic and environmental practices. As in the cases of politics already discussed and the geostrategy covered in Chapter 4, these efforts are, however, only likely to bear positive fruit if they incorporate and learn from their historical precursors.

THE BASE ECONOMY SINCE 1945

The critical role of economics in determining the scale and form of US military bases throughout Japan's Southwest Island Chain is all too often forgotten behind a more geomilitarily oriented focus upon the power and awe of US forces and their accompanying machinery.[1] In reality, however, the American war machine's presence on Okinawa is determined primarily by economic interests and has been, to a large extent, since its inception after the Battle of Okinawa in 1945 (Selden 1971: 50). What has changed dramatically, though, is the extent to which the bases on Okinawa no longer form such a central part of the local economy. In that regard, the reduction of direct financial reliance upon US military deployments and activity can be considered as one area of relatively positive change, as Okinawa's unwanted status as a potential flashpoint for major conflict is somewhat reduced because of the US military's downsized economic footprint.[2] However, such an assessment must

1 An example of this military focus can be found in Robson & Kusumoto (2022).

2 An assessment is provided by Okinawa Prefecture's official website under the title "Beigun kichi to okinawa keizai ni tsuite" [Regarding the Okinawan economy and American bases], https://www.pref.okinawa.jp/kensei/shisaku/1014345/1014346.html.

be qualified by the compensating factor that there is now a concerted effort from the central GoJ to make a geographical shift southwestward, officially termed the *nansei shifuto* within formal Japanese government rhetoric and publications. This includes the ostensive aim of increasing JSDF bases on Okinawa (Kurihara 2019).

In that regard, in order to gain a nuanced understanding of the relationship between broader localized economics and the base economy in the prefecture, we first need to review its origins. This traces back to the conclusion of the Pacific War, which utterly obliterated the Okinawan economy, culminating in the catastrophic Battle of Okinawa. Furthermore, it bears reemphasizing here that the socio-economic devastation was not only a result of the bombardment by invading Allied forces but also a function of wartime exploitation on the part of the IJA (Siddle 1998). Japanese forces systematically co-opted and exploited those locals who were of an age capable of productive labour, confiscated crops and other food sources, and prevented further arable and farmland usage by occupying extensive parts of Okinawa's narrow landmass, as well as effectively ending all pre-war forms of nascent tourism that existed in the prefecture. As these practices of military economy intensified around the islands in the build-up to the Battle of Okinawa, many of the local population were already barely at the level of subsistence when the Americans landed their 77th infantry division on the Kerama Islands in April of 1945 to initiate an all-out assault. By the time the battle ended three months later, most civilians who had not been killed in the crossfire were either actually or on the verge of starving to death, meaning there was effectively no functioning domestic economy to speak of (Feifer 2000).

The rebooting of Okinawa's economy was, in that sense, at first driven almost entirely by US aid and investment into the region, partly as a functionality of the US-led wars in Korea and later Vietnam.[3] This included the expropriation of huge areas of land on Okinawa Main Island and its immediate off-islands to construct and upgrade military bases and air strips that had been hastily laid down in preparation for

3 This process is documented by the specialist blog, Kainan Corporation, through the post "Okinawa no gunyōchi no rekishi (zenhen)" [The history of American military facilities on Okinawa], https://www.kainanco.jp/blog/1236/.

the expected Allied land invasion of mainland Japan that never came. Today's MCAS Futenma is a flagship example of this (Nishiyama 2022: 546). Initially the base was built for launching bombing raids directly onto the four main Japanese islands, but the American blockade of Japan – itself a prime example of economic warfare at its most brutally effective – meant that the Pacific War ended without the need for extensive use of the airstrip at Futenma. That led to its expansion and redevelopment in the immediate postwar period for use in other wars on the Korean Peninsula and later in Southeast Asia. It also resulted in local residents being forcibly removed from the lands occupied by their homes at the point of bayonets and bulldozers to build what has ultimately become today's vast MCAS Futenma base (Sakurazawa 2016: 20). These displaced local people were in some cases paid a nominal, absurdly small lease fee for renting their land to the Americans. They were, thereafter, joined by thousands of other impoverished Okinawans living in the area, who little-by-little constructed the now 90,000-strong city of Ginowan around the base. Indeed, in-migration to Ginowan rapidly accelerated on account of MCAS Futenma being one of the few immediate postwar sites of substantial economic activity that offered a means to generate income through employment (Nishiyama 2022).

The reasons for the urbanization process converging around the military facility of what essentially remains to this day an occupying army were, therefore, primarily economic. This was because the MCAS Futenma base, as well as others throughout Okinawa's main island, provided opportunities for paid remuneration within multiple industries and spin-off economies. These included the sale of goods and services as well as the physical (re)construction of runways and other base infrastructure itself.[4] Nevertheless, as discussed further below, the construction of bases on Okinawa in this way became representative of how a small number of mostly mainland Japanese construction companies were able to make huge financial profits through the *development* of postwar base projects. For many of the locals on the other hand, who in the main had previously been farmers, fishers or other primary industry

4 This phenomenon of "base economies" is not limited to Okinawa but rather it is something common to most of the network of US bases around the world. For further discussion, see Enloe (2014).

workers, there was little choice other than to join the base economy, especially given that much of their workable lands had in effect been fenced off and turned into bases (Junkerman 2016b). At Futenma it created the foundations of what has been branded the world's most dangerous base, with today's Ginowan City hugging the perimeter fences in what we have already noted is far closer proximity than would be legally allowed on any equivalent military facility on the US mainland. In the case of MCAS Futenma, this includes backing onto schools, a university and countless other residential buildings that are literally adjacent to the base's exterior fence.[5]

Given the collapse of Okinawa's wartime society and grinding poverty among the decimated civilian population that survived, it is unsurprising, then, that the broader Okinawan political economy came to rely heavily upon both direct and indirect investment via these American security facilities. The bases not only provided desperately needed jobs within them, customers for services around them and donations from wealthy stakeholders invested into them; they were also essential sources of bureaucratic justification for approving large-scale construction and public works projects. Hence, the construction industry and other related commercial businesses were able to take financial advantage of calls to contribute towards the revitalizing of the local economy. At the same time, this process came at great cost to the local environment, traditional ways of life (mostly based around fishing and subsistence farming) and cultural heritage. The transformation included concrete changes to the physical shape of Okinawa's natural coastline and inhabitable spaces (Urashima 2009). In this regard, while debate continues regarding the coexistent positive and negative impacts upon today's Okinawan economy and society, from the immediate postwar period until reversion back to Japanese rule in 1972 Okinawa can quite credibly be described as one of the world's most emblematic examples of a base economy.

This included a dependency ratio of up to 30 per cent of prefectural revenue through the early postwar years.[6] However, what is often

5 How views of the bases have changed on Okinawa as a result of this reality is informatively discussed in Cena (2022).

6 Further details can be found through the Washington, DC office of the Okinawa Prefecture; see, for example, Okinawa Prefecture Government (2016).

underevaluated by those who seek to criticize the changes brought about by such massive base-building projects along ethical lines is that this asymmetrical reliance upon the US military did help significantly to stabilize the islands' socio-economic situation from an administrative perspective. In that sense, dependence was preferable to abandonment. Related aid and investment also tangibly improved living standards. What is more, despite understandable protest and domestic discontentment with the disproportionately concentrated human rights abuses committed by US military servicemembers, when compared to militarist Japanese rule and the Battle of Okinawa itself the overall level of violent conflict within the prefecture was substantively reduced during these early Cold War years (Aldous 2003: 485). In these respects, the foundations of contemporary Okinawa's functioning economic, social and administrative structures were effectively created while under American rule as a US protectorate with extraterritorial status (Takizawa 1971: 496).

On the flip side, because of its almost total lack of administrative self-autonomy, and therefore inability to oppose US foreign or domestic GoJ policy, Okinawa in multiple forms became a key launch site for the prosecution of American wars in East and Southeast Asian theatres. This underlying function was repeatedly justified in the context of the Cold War fight against communism and the promotion of liberal democracy as the backbone for a robust economy, which was supposed to be attained through US-dictated rules, values and restructuring (Koikari 2015). Furthermore, in the same way in which US military campaigns were driven from Okinawa partly by the huge financial vested interests that form part of what President Dwight Eisenhower famously described as the military-industrial complex, they also stimulated Okinawa's recovering but fragile economy.[7] Nevertheless, they were set up largely to serve the interests of a US-backed iron triangle that still rules Japan today, comprising big business, the bureaucracy and Tokyo's ruling LDP. In addition, spin-off industries allowed the long-tolerated Japanese *yakuza*, or organized crime syndicates, to establish a firm foothold on the island in tandem with historically

7 The full script of the president's speech can be found in the National Archives under "President Dwight D. Eisenhower's farewell address (1961)".

localized organized criminal groups (see Yellow Glasses 2019). This manifested itself in *entertainment* districts that sprung up around the bases on Okinawa from which troops would be rotated to and from the battlefields of Indochina and elsewhere. The result was the creation of so-called *amemura*, or American villages. Indeed, a somewhat diversified, gentrified and transformed form of these are still present in Okinawa's Chatan Town and vicinity on the islands today. During the active US wars of the pre-reversion era in particular, sex and narcotics industries, as well as underworld crime, thereby flourished as part of a lucrative grey economy.[8]

These grey-zone economic activities were, indeed, an essential part of many locals' means to make a living. Controversially, however, they created a shadow economy that involved multiple *yakuza* families, who established their competing strongholds within the prefecture. They also included the running of an extensive network of prostitution facilities to service off-duty American military personnel, in addition to some tourists and locals. Not only was this illegal and bound up with extortion and violent crime, it also involved the deplorable practice of effectively (although usually informally) buying young women and girls from their families to be used in sexual semi-slavery (Kikuchi 2002: 94). A further cruel irony of this industry rests in the fact that having supposedly been liberated from the oppression of Japanese militarism, which included coercing Okinawan women into sexual slavery as part of the so-called comfort women system designed to satisfy members of the IJA, the following generation of young female islanders were now being cajoled into a similar situation despite the oversight of a supposedly functioning liberal democracy. This situation was created by a mixture of gangsters, occupying soldiers and the young women's own families, the last of which relied upon the income of sex work to support family finances when few other sources of reliable income could be secured. To compound the situation, these practices came in addition to widespread sexual violence committed against local women by military personnel, itself partly a function of economic pressures that led to Okinawa being used as a relatively cost-efficient element of the US-led Cold War and its associated military-industrial congressional complex (Reed-Fouts 2021: 24).

8 Further details of these practices are documented in Mitchel (2022).

Elsewhere in the prefecture, the situation varied wildly from island to island, and even north to south on Okinawa Main Island. This disparity was typified by unequal investment and impacted by one-off mega-projects directed from mainland Japanese consortiums, such as that behind the 1975 Okinawa Expo, hosted on the relatively remote northern Motobu Peninsula (Blaxell 2010). In many cases, including those of the next largest islands, Ishigaki and Miyakojima, by contrast, the absence of bases resulted in a less tumultuous and more gradual development of the local economy, mostly revolving around tourism. Although there was seen to be little need for Washington to construct new bases on these outlying island clusters – given the priority focus on facing off against the Soviet Union from Hokkaido rather than against China from the Ryukyu Islands – funds still had to be designated from the US government budget to ensure that welfare, education and administrative organization were maintained. There was, nonetheless, uneven development across the prefecture and the rapid establishment, or revival, of tourist industries where the absence of bases left a physical and economic space for them to flourish (Nguyen 2012). Further out still, on the prefecture's most southwesterly island of Yonaguni, close proximity with Taiwan facilitated an explosion of informal trade in goods between Taiwanese coastal communities and the rapidly growing on-island population. However, these activities were quickly targeted and shut down by the US administration as a potential point of extra-legal economic activity and infiltration from outside of American oversight (Ouchi 2002). Thereafter, partly as a response to these intra-prefectural disparities and irregularities, and later in preparation for Okinawa's reversion to mainland Japan, over time the Prefectural Government authorities were standardized and economic relationships of all kinds more rigorously regulated.

The reversion process itself can also be seen largely as a function of economics. Indeed, this aspect of Okinawa's switch to Japanese rule is often overlooked or underplayed, including by much of the, mostly left-leaning, scholarship on Okinawa that seeks to depict the events of 1972 as the culmination of a long-running popular struggle for emancipation from US oppression and human rights abuses (Tanji 2006). Such narratives have a tendency to omit or misrepresent the extent to which many Okinawan citizens simply wanted a piece of the Japanese economic miracle that they saw taking off on mainland Japan during the 1960s and 1970s (Mason 2016: 29). Meanwhile, the Americans needed a way to cut their burgeoning overseas military costs caused by massive overinvestment in costly wars fought and abetted throughout the Indo-Pacific and elsewhere. In particular, the US administration was looking to find an off-ramp from the expensive, unpopular and protracted Vietnam War. Within this context, transferring the administration of Okinawa – and thereby all of its associated welfare and infrastructural expenses – to the Japanese government looked like a favourable option (Kim 1973: 1028–9). This was even more the case given that Washington was in a position to dictate the key condition of reversion as being granted only if it retained all of its military facilities on Okinawa at cost to the Japanese taxpayer under the pretext of an *omoiyari yosan*, or sympathy budget.[9] Furthermore, US negotiators could claim to do so while promoting democracy with reference to the widespread support among locals gained for reversion, despite the fact that a majority of citizens did not want to see the military bases retained.

In the years that followed, after initial euphoria over having *won* reversion and being able to look forward expectantly to an improved lifestyle and standard of living at *hondo nami*, or in line with mainland Japan, discontentment began to grow among the local population. This came as they witnessed an enduring economic gap between themselves and those living on Japan's four largest islands.[10] Despite subsidized aid packages, stimulus from central government and specialized local tax exemptions designed to boost multisector industry growth, this gap included lagging rates of income, educational achievement and job opportunities, all of which persist to this day.[11] Furthermore, because of lifestyle changes that increased fast food consumption and reduced

9 Explanation of this practice can be found on the website of the Peace Studies Association of Japan, including "100 no ronten: 5. sengo nichibei kankei no naka de okinawa wa nan datta no deshō ka" [100 points of debate: no. 5, how was Okinawa manifest within postwar Japan–US relations?], https://www.psaj.org/100points5/.

10 The extent of this gap is detailed in Nihon Keizai Shimbun (2022).

11 Detailed rankings of various wealth and achievement indicators can be found online at "Statistics Japan: prefecture comparisons", https://www.nikkei.com/article/DGXZQOJC07BZ90X00C23A7000000/.

physical exercise, endemic relative poverty was coupled with an actual decline in the health standards of younger generations whose ancestors had once achieved notoriety for being the world's longest living population (DW 2022). These negative trends were coupled with a growing perception that central government was continuing to exploit and discriminate against those from the Ryukyu Islands. Nowhere could this have been more apparent than at the 1975 Okinawa Expo. In flagrant disregard of local interests, Japanese mainland companies constructed a huge event site on and offshore of Motobu Peninsula, ensuring that profits were extracted, maximized and largely taken out of the prefectural economy to be funnelled back into corporate coffers in Tokyo and elsewhere. This even included the physical construction and subsequent dismantling of a floating sea world and its contents, which resulted in short-term, poorly paid manual labour but a dearth of meaningful long-term local jobs (Blaxell 2010).

This inglorious spectacle itself came after what could be described as a commercial flashpoint on Okinawa. Thereby, initial pre- and post-reversion attempts by major US enterprises to use the administrative changeover of 1972 to enter into the rapidly expanding Japanese market via Okinawa were actively blocked by Tokyo's government. This was done through instrumentalizing legislation in a form that can only be deemed as amounting to exclusionary economic nationalism (Howell 2000: 244). Thereafter, the exclusion of US companies limited external investment at the same time as discriminatory practices by the GoJ against the prefecture remained. Nevertheless, as Japan boomed in the 1980s so too did Okinawa's economy in relative terms. Tourism was obviously a key part of this. The prefecture's stunning marine scenery and warm waters attracted increasingly wealthy mainland visitors and investors. Meanwhile, successive Japanese national governments flush with cash were able to increase the *ikkatsu kōfukin*, or one-off subsidy payments, given to Okinawa Prefecture as compensation for hosting bases. This allowed for the massive expansion of local infrastructural development programmes to boost a broad base of industry sectors and increase overall employment rates. Along with the bases (*kichi*), this resulted in tourism (*kankō*) and construction (*kensetsu*) becoming the final two of the three "big K" industries established on Okinawa. The last two industries were hit hard by the knock-on effects of Japan's real estate bubble bursting in 1991, but they have nevertheless, along with the public administration sector, remained key segments in the backbone of the Okinawan economy. At the same time, in some regards the linkage between these three core industries and the contested geopolitical aspects of governance over Okinawa cannot be ignored. This is because, in combination, they play a key role in dictating and maintaining the status quo between Japan's iron triangle (LDP, bureaucracy and big business) and the US authorities and their interests. They are also active agents in and of themselves in the destruction of Okinawa's fragile ecosystems (Aldrich 1999). This is most evidently manifest by way of facilitating land reclamation and base construction projects.

BIG BUSINESS: CONSTRUCTION, CONCRETE AND GRAVEL

As expertly detailed by Gerald Figal, the development of Okinawa's tourist industry has been beset by controversy, corruption and red tape (Figal 2012). This is despite being the sector that one might expect to be far and away the biggest business in town given Okinawa Prefecture's characterization as the "Hawaii of Japan". Many of these difficulties have been exacerbated in large part by the dominance of the construction industry throughout the islands. This particularly pertains to concrete and gravel companies, whose influence runs deep and whose interests do not necessarily always align with those of the commercial tourism sector. For example, the construction of highways, bridges and concrete tunnels, although providing access to key sites, destroys the very natural beauty of the islands that many tourists come to see. This has been countered somewhat in recent decades by the construction of reclaimed land sites that are developed into expensive urban suburbs, complete with shopping malls and artificial beaches.[12] However, the extent to which such projects are, once again, largely owned by mainland Japanese companies is striking. In that sense, the postwar evolution

12 The southwest coastal districts of Toyosaki, Nishizaki and Shiozaki are flagship examples of this kind of development, having completely reshaped the area's once natural coastline.

of the construction industry on Okinawa and the structural power that it wields is in many ways reflective of Japan's national structures of governance towards the prefecture.

These illustrate the protracted colonial-style economic relationship that mainland Japan continues to maintain with its remotest regional territory.[13] The financially driven aspects of this dynamic also further highlight the close linkage, or revolving door, retained between big business, politicians and bureaucrats among Japan's elite.[14] As noted above, this perpetuates the model of a so-called iron triangle, which is exemplified, albeit in a microcosm, on Okinawa. Notwithstanding legitimate career progressions, this involves what could be interpreted as a kind of systemized collusion, whereby former employees, close associates and industrial sponsors of politicians are awarded large public sector contracts for infrastructure projects that are approved, administered or overseen by the bureaucratic arms of local government. Some of these cosy relationships are convened at the level of the Prefectural Government as well as local municipalities, including under the authority of sections designated as *tochi kaihatsu kōsha*, or public urban development corporations.[15] The result is often the fast-tracking of lucrative projects of dubious broader benefit to local communities. Even if not actually illegal or collusive, public–private collaborations have been particularly prominent in this regard, especially when developed without proper consideration for local environments or historic scenery. The case of Itoman City's eyesore hotel complex along the previously scenic Nashiro Beach site is an exemplar case in point, though only one of many such sites throughout the prefecture (Figure 3.1). The two massive hotel buildings constructed there – aesthetically resembling something between a former Soviet-style public housing estate and a large hospital complex when viewed from most rear angles – sit amid an otherwise idyllic and picturesque natural rural coastline.

Okinawa's construction industry has continued to grow in this way. Not least, it has done so as a means through which to channel the

13 The depth of this relationship was explained to the author in a 16 May 2023 interview with Yasukatsu Matsushima at Ryukoku University, Kyoto.

14 For discussion of the revolving door system, see Japan Times (2017).

15 These are led by the Prefectural Okinawa Ken Tochi Kaihatsu Kōsha (Okinawa Prefecture Public Land Development Corporation).

Figure 3.1 Commercial hotel developments along Okinawa's pristine natural coasts

Source: iStock.

compensatory *ikkatsu kōfukin* payments, which, in addition to the compensation provided for bases, are ostensibly transferred from central to local government to level-up Okinawa's status as one of Japan's poorest prefectures. However, neither of these hazards – poverty and military base hosting – are sufficiently compensated by the lump sums offered in this way. Rather, by subtly but significantly increasing and decreasing the annual amount allocated as *ikkatsu kōfukin* within central government budgets, Tokyo is able to in effect reward compliant behaviour by the Prefectural Government and punish aberrance. For example, former Prefectural Governor Nakaima Hirokazu, who acquiesced under pressure to approve landfill for the new base construction site at Henoko, was given an increased budget, while his successor, Takeshi Onaga, as well as incumbent Tamaki Denny, both of whom have resolutely attempted to block construction of the facility, saw their annual *ikkatsu kōfukin* slashed.

This was seemingly as a punishment for their opposition to policies dictated by the ruling LDP.[16] Such an overt and centralized carrot and stick approach, using the contraction and expansion of the money supply, only serves to reinforce accusations of economic weaponization by the GoJ over Okinawa. In addition, these aspects are further exacerbated by the fact that, ultimately, the system allows those in positions of relative wealth and power to redirect public funds into the hands of private companies that carry out the construction projects. Frequently, these are parented, owned or directed by actors form the Japanese mainland. In other words, rather than significantly raising the standard of living for most Okinawans, the Japanese taxpayers' money that funds the *ikkatsu kōfukin* is mostly being transferred from public mainland coffers into private mainland enterprises via convivial public–private commercial relations acted out on Okinawa. The result is a system that incentivizes the creation of massive construction projects, many of which are not strictly speaking necessary. They do, however, serve to employ large numbers of local workers at minimum or low rates of pay. Meanwhile, patterns of employment are generally temporary and precarious while enriching the employers, who are awarded these public contracts in an environment of relatively low-risk (because of the near certainty that public funds will underwrite them) and high-reward (because of the amounts involved) investment into their related industries (Kerr 2001).

Concrete is perhaps the industry that offers the starkest example of this phenomenon. From a four-lane bypass along Itoman City's relatively quiet southwest coast to two deserted highways on tiny Izena Island, a giant bridge and airport access road in the Kerama Islands that serves two communities of fewer than 1,000 residents each, and whole new artificial beaches and towns reclaimed in rectangles from the sea, not to mention new military facilities, concrete is everywhere on Okinawa.[17] Importantly, while many of these projects do encounter some civil opposition, it is usually of a highly limited nature, particularly as many on the islands have little alternative other than continued employment in the construction sector and view infrastructure projects

16 For details of this seemingly punitive tightening of the public coffers, see Akahata Shimbun (2022).

17 For discussion of how the concrete business functions, see Joi (2008).

as a sign of development. This is not surprising given the limited vocational opportunities outside of these sectors and their promotion by public offices, private firms and mass media, who also tend to promote projects as modern developments that will enhance, rather than detract from, Okinawa's considerable attraction as a go-to destination.[18] Such depictions include numerous construction projects undertaken within the tourist sector. In that regard, there is some evidence that concretization is actually viewed positively in terms of attracting mainland Asian tourists, as trends suggest this subsection predominantly target modern urban shopping at Okinawa's multiple new duty-free malls, convenience of airport access and single-location, inclusive, resort-type hotels, rather than the particular aesthetics of a natural coastline or diverse options of ecotourism.[19] Nevertheless, there are obviously limits to the ongoing concreting-over process given Okinawa's geographically limited size. Indeed, this rapid industrial expansion is already bumping up against a variety of competing economic and environmental interests. These also contain a concerning international component, as discussed below.

COMPETING COMMERCIAL INTERESTS

The limits of space and differing visions of ideal land usage outlined above, as well as the disparity between different islands within the prefecture, are not insignificant causes of friction in and of themselves on Okinawa. However, the greatest sources of economic conflict are predominantly to be found floating upon, swimming amid and buried beneath the ocean surrounding the Ryukyu Islands. These can be crudely divided into three categories: shipping, fisheries and energy. The complex specifics manifest within each of these sectors now converges around a single flashpoint, as competition over all three of these major

18 These are even largely endorsed by local news media that generally oppose mainland vested interests; see, for example, Okinawa Times (2022b).

19 These tourist tastes are reflected in Okinawa Prefecture's public survey statistics, "Gaikokujin kankōkyaku manzoku chōsa" [Foreign tourists satisfaction survey]: https://www.pref.okinawa.lg.jp/_res/projects/default_project/_page_/001/020/321/h22inbound_survey_report.pdf.

industries, which are vital to Japan's, China's and Taiwan's economic security, intersect at the disputed Senkaku Islands.

Although often depicted in contemporary IR literature as either of key geostrategic or, symbolically, political importance, it can be argued that this trilateral dispute is ultimately driven by resource-led conflicts of interest (see Konishi 2011). China's contemporary official claims to these uninhabited islets, for instance, were irrefutably initiated only after a United Nations Convention on the Law of the Sea report in 1967 revealed the likely presence of extensive natural resources beneath the surrounding seas. These include oil, liquid gas and other minerals buried under the seabed, for which exploitation and governance rights are seemingly open to international arbitration.[20] Initially, this was a source of hope and potential cooperation as Sino-Japanese relations warmed in step with Beijing's increasing need for, and reliance upon, Tokyo to provide the official development assistance and foreign direct investment that helped transform its post-Maoist economy. Political support from both sides, including a famous statement by former Chinese Premier Deng Xiaoping, to shelve the dispute for future generations to solve duly followed.[21] Since that time, however, as China's economic and geomilitary strength has grown relative to that of Japan's, the appetite for joint exploitation of these undersea resources has waned in place of a more unilateral position adopted by the PRC. Meanwhile, competition because of overfishing of the area's dwindling fish stocks has intensified.

Further to this, as explored in greater detail throughout Chapter 4, exaggerated and unilateral claims from all sides concerning fishing rights have served to escalate tensions at the level of international security. These disputes remain unresolved and are an enduring source of potential future conflict. In addition, there is also an increasingly explicit clash of interests regarding transition through and around the Senkaku islets, as well as other sea lanes throughout the Ryukyu Islands

---

20 The pertaining legal provisions for this are stipulated on p. 63 of the United Nations' 1970 Convention on the Law of the Sea.

21 The CCP's Ministry of Foreign Affairs of the PRC still display's Deng's statement on its official website, "Set aside dispute and pursue joint development" (2014), https://www.mfa.gov.cn/eng/zy/wjls/3604_665547/202405/t20240531_11367540.html.

chain. In other words, the nautical arteries of maritime trade routes are becoming fiercely contested (McDevitt *et al.* 2012). Here, too, as China's comparative strength grows, it may seek to further control the commercial transit of cargoes that traverse the area. There is additional evidence of this from the skies above the same seascape, where Beijing has unilaterally designated an Air Defence Identification Zone (ADIZ) (MOFA 2013). When compared with China's constricting of major maritime trade throughways in the South China Sea, this may seem like comparatively small change. Nonetheless, in the event of a Taiwan contingency or other heightened competition between China, Japan and the US, shipping routes both around the disputed zones and between inhabited Okinawan islands are likely to become sites of intensified economic competition, as extended supply logistics become central to sustaining live populations and military campaigns.[22] This includes discussion that ocean-bound passages could be subjected to full or limited blockades by either side.[23] Furthermore, as demonstrated by the punitive measures periodically exercised by Beijing towards Taipei and the supposedly health-related restrictions imposed during the Covid-19 pandemic, the CCP might readily decide to threaten or implement localized economic sanctions by boycotting Okinawan tourist sites and commercial centres in response to any perceived provocation by the collective US–Japan Security Alliance.

THE ECONOMIC COSTS OF AN ENVIRONMENTAL FLASHPOINT

Against this backdrop of strategic US–China and Sino-Japanese rivalries being played out as a function of competing political economies, Okinawa has already become a flashpoint for international militant attempts regarding environmental conservation. If one considers the gravity of current climate crises and endemic pollution throughout the Indo-Pacific, the ongoing devastation of Okinawa's fragile environment

22 This was confirmed to the author in a 24 April 2023 interview with an anonymous former US military logistics expert in Okinawa City.

23 Various scenarios are discussed in Mukai (2023).

must be given due weight in any cost–benefit analysis of the region. This includes seeking to understand the economic drivers and implications, which are all the more significant as Okinawa boasts the lucrative allure of an incredible nine UNESCO world heritage sites, in addition to its coral-filled seas. These are central to its appeal as a tourist attraction, but they also play a seemingly contradictory role in both agitating and mitigating legal disputes between US, Japanese and Okinawan authorities and the local population. The agitation comes because of competition over the highly limited physical space occupied by fragile ecosystems and sights of natural beauty. The mitigation draws from proactive collaborative efforts regarding environmental protection and formalized management that can serve to build trust, which can in turn then be linked to other areas of cooperation.[24] Either way, these complex aspects of economic contestation and convergence are inextricably linked to an increasingly grave degree of environmental destruction throughout the islands.

Nowhere is this more evident than at Henoko. Construction of the new base, ostensibly being built as a replacement facility for MCAS Futenma, has been the subject of multiple international environmental court cases. All of these have favoured the side seeking to block construction (Tanji 2008: 477). Yet here too, economic interests represented by mainland construction companies, private security firms and government-backed military contractors have ensured that the development and environmental destruction continues.[25] The dispute over this new base is, as with so many aspects of Okinawa's politics, economics and security, complicated in nature. Therein, it is more than simply a case of competing values, or coral versus concrete. Rather, it is emblematic of the wider complexities that surround a range of disputes on Okinawa, many of which have historically embedded economic origins relating to the vested interests discussed above. They also have

24 One of these initiatives is led by the Okinawa Environmental Justice Project as detailed in their public statement, "OEJP statement on Japan–U.S. bilateral cooperation for the World Heritage Yambaru Forest", https://okinawaejp.blogspot.com/2023/07/oejp-statement-on-japan-us-bilateral.html.

25 For a critique, see Tokyo Shimbun (2022).

significant future implications for the new green economy.[26] In the case of Henoko, as a small and relatively remote village settlement towards the north of Okinawa Main Island, a reconceptualization of economic security may be required to achieve this. Commercial activity and growth were strongest during the American military campaigns of the 1960s, as servicemembers were rolled in and out of the adjacent Camp Schwab on their way to deployments in Southeast Asia. This provided the demand for local hospitality industries and other services that were heavily reliant upon a steady flow of US dollars into the local economy. Such income streams thereby supplemented traditional trades such as fishing and farming, neither of which had been intensive enough to destroy the local environment. In that regard, though, it is worth noting that pollution first became problematic in the area as a function primarily of imported US detergents that poisoned fish and coral through run-off, as well as chemicals discharged from military operations and activities (Dudden 2019). Today, in taking advantage of the current global wave of commercially based green initiatives, there are nascent signs that traditional Okinawan industries may be rejuvenated through new, supposedly sound, sustainable techno-agricultural innovations. In addition to more sustainable fishing and permaculture farming, these are set to include an expansion of coral regeneration projects.[27]

As such, although often surprisingly indifferent to environmental issues,[28] it is evident that local residents are not oblivious to the extensive changes taking place in their surrounding environment and its relationship to their economy. However, as with elsewhere across the prefecture, many imported products that have caused harm to local freshwater and saltwater environments, as well as the fragile *inō*, or tidal plain, which is situated in the coastal zone between the two, have been actively purchased and discharged as much by local citizens as foreign military personnel. For example, outflow from household washing

26 This was addressed at the 26 May 2023 World Economic Forum session, "How Asia's green economy will transform the world in the next decade".

27 The Okinawa Institute of Science and Technology (OIST) provides updates of these initiatives; see OIST (2018).

28 This observation was confirmed by residents of Okinawa's central regions in interviews on 4 March 2023.

powder imports that released bleach into Okinawa's river basins and bays destroyed much of the marine life in these fragile ecosystems.[29] Moreover, it was evidently indigenous Okinawans as much as American soldiers who were prioritizing economic over environmental concerns in their relentless use of these products, as well as in utilizing pesticides and petrochemicals across a range of primary industries. In that sense, these changes to the local environment and economy have to be understood within their appropriate historical context, amid a pre-environmentalist era. This is in contrast with the current battle over Henoko's development, which pits Japanese central government, local law enforcement and the vested interests of the industries already identified above – including gravel, concrete and construction more generally – in a clash with the Prefectural Government, prefecture-wide public opinion and international environmental campaigners (see Asahi Shimbun 2021).

Among this complex set of competing interests, a majority of Henoko's residents buck the prefecture-wide trend of opposition against the base by supporting construction of the new facility within their municipality on the grounds that it aids economic rejuvenation (Williams 2013: 959). Yet they appear to have afforded little consideration to the economic costs of base construction and its resulting environmental damage in the longer term. These elements may well outstrip potential short-term financial gains secured as a function of larger numbers of military servicemembers and their families moving into the area. This is even more likely to be the case when considering the Prefectural Government's determination to exploit all available legal channels in order to further protract the situation and delay completion of the new base (Nagy 2022). In other words, an extended cost–benefit analysis has seemingly been prematurely determined based on historical evaluations of how one relatively populated base (Camp Schwab) formerly contributed to the village economy. In contrast, endangered species of rare marine life, such as the dugong, or sea manatee, as well as the rich coral-filled environment within which they live, has extensive allure to increasingly environmentally aware cohorts of tourists visiting Okinawa (Nakazawa

29 This claim was made in a 4 July 2005 interview with then Itoman City Mayor Yamazato Chōsei.

2021: 13). Many of these would-be disposable income-carrying visitors are less likely to visit an area that contains a large and noisy military base and runway catering to vertical take-off war machines, and even less so an ongoing construction site!

Yet if effectively framed, strategized and marketed towards diversifying economic interests, Okinawa probably offers an ideal location from which to rapidly expand an already growing ecotourism sector. Such growth looks set to combine and integrate with nascent scientific development projects affiliated to leading universities on the islands, as well as being combined with promotion as a renowned sports Mecca. The latter has been skilfully marketed under the banner of "Sports Islands Okinawa", which includes promoting sports tourism enjoyed in the balmy climate and the hosting of multiple professional sports teams and competitions. Hence, visionary thinking and strong leadership are likely to be key variables if these initiatives are to be elevated to the level of prioritization that has historically been given to military bases. Thus far, the latter have mostly been put first in the name of deterrence and security, even at the cost of massive environmental degradation. Conversely, in order to ease tensions around the serious pollution and non-sustainable natural land usage issues facing Okinawa, economic security and improved regional tourism may have to be more forcefully promoted (Mason 2023: 131). To be effective, these sectors will probably need to incorporate public and private sector actors, as well as the US military where possible, so that development projects and initiatives are viewed as something complementary to, and relying upon, environmental conservation, rather than being in competition with green causes.

The conceptual scope of these biodiverse aspects also varies. In that regard, hitherto efforts to widen and infuse environmental causes with a more publicly understood discourse around what would make economic and ecological sense for the islands' future have been limited. For instance, at the postgraduate Okinawa Institute for Science and Technology (OIST), the prefecture is hosting a range of world-class higher education and professional scientist groups conducting cutting-edge research into marine biosciences. In spite of this, however, the facility is strikingly underemphasized in the Prefectural Government's official promotion of Okinawa, despite the fact that OIST has considerable links to lucrative industries, as well as to prominent foreign academics and investors.[30] At least four of the other seven universities on Okinawa at the time of writing also conduct research relevant to promoting environmentally sound initiatives for economic development. In these regards, if more strategically managed, Okinawa's economy would appear to contain all the elements needed to transform it into something like a scaled-down version of Taiwan, in terms of developing a broad base of diverse local industries. This is made particularly evident when it comes to becoming a centre for the innovation and production of leading environmental technologies. These could not only help to secure the prefecture's future prosperity through broadening the economic base but also boost regional integration, incentivize corporate backing for the islands' ecological protection and disincentivize invasion and military attack (including from China) because extensive investment by any state-backed enterprise would increase the economic costs it incurred if attacking sites on Okinawa.

ECONOMIC DIVERSIFICATION AND VULNERABILITY: OKINAWA VERSUS TAIWAN

The preceding discussion suggests that the Okinawan economy is rich in potential but also fragile as the source of complex conflicts of interest sandwiched between a range of powerful domestic and external actors. An examination of multiple sectors, however, indicates that it does contain the key elements needed to grow into a unique substate hub for ecotourism, island sports and marine sciences, as well as technological research and development. It is hard to deny that the endemic vested interests of a narrow group of mostly mainland-based industries, in combination with limited geographical space caused by an overloading of US military bases, exacerbates and constraints further development of the economy. Nevertheless, a comparison with Taiwan – one of the region's most dynamic island economies – offers an intriguing line of investigation into how, if imbued with a visionary developmentalist strategy and sufficient political will, dramatic transformations might rapidly be realized (Lauridsen 2014). It also illustrates the degree to

30 These were detailed in Nagamine (2022).

which a diversified and value-added economy greatly reduces vulnerability in terms of realizing both economic and political security. What is more, despite its relatively small size and lack of administrative autonomy, Okinawa has a wealth of subsectors, including those relating to its standout natural environment. In response, there are signs that the prefecture will aim to carve out commercially driven regional niches that could actually surpass even those established successfully by Taipei.

In terms of realizing the development of new niche industries and markets for Okinawa, it is clear from the details of the Prefectural Government's strategic 21st Century Basic Plans developed across a range of key sectors that the prefectural authorities in Naha, along with local private sector companies and entrepreneurs, have in some respects moved ahead of Tokyo's central government (Okinawa Prefectural Government 2012, 2023). They have also learned from Taiwan's playbook in terms of developing business relations with mainland China under a banner that essentially mirrors Beijing's much maligned rhetoric on market-driven win–win strategies to deepen and strengthen regional relations (MFA PRC 2023). In fact, while some concerns have duly been raised at the local level regarding independent initiatives by the Okinawa Prefectural Government to advance commercial exchange with nearby Chinese provinces, such efforts have been largely endorsed within the public sphere on Okinawa. In particular, Okinawa Prefectural Governor Denny Tamaki has led the initiative to promote a socio-economic network of local politicians, business actors, academics and community leaders at the regional level, as a way of boosting localized economic growth while at the same time indirectly engaging more proactively with both Taipei and Beijing. Indeed, the local government argues that this approach is likely to promote integration and reduce the likelihood of potential conflict (Okinawa Prefectural Government 2022: 9).

However, unlike the Taiwanese case of de facto self-governance as an independently functioning state, when economic and political interests are not aligned at the national level these localized efforts can be rapidly undermined or overruled by Japan's central government, because of Okinawa's complete lack of devolution. In other words, despite popular claims to the rights of self-governance under Article 95 of Japan's constitution, Okinawa lacks practical legislative, executive and legal powers of self-determination (Constitute Project 2018: 17). This means that if the hawkish side of the ruling LDP decides to take a combative stance towards China and interfere in localized trade-based exchanges between Okinawan islands and elsewhere on the grounds that they appease or encourage Beijing, they can readily do so with almost complete impunity. For instance, this has been observed in the case of Yonaguni Island's circumscribed relations with the city of Hualien, as well as widespread criticism of Governor Tamaki for his overtures towards the Xi Jinping regime (Endo 2023; Nakazawa 2023). In addition to national and local bureaucracies cancelling permits and slashing budgets that could facilitate these more independent Okinawan activities, formal provisions and legal procedures can also be implemented by Tokyo's executive and legislature, often working in close lockstep with their partners in the judiciary to curtail acts of self-governance that might be indicative of, or lead to, greater economic autonomy (Okubo 2015).

Yet historically speaking Okinawa has credible claims to equivalent, if not greater, legitimacy when it comes to strengthening ties with mainland China than does Taiwan. The government in Taipei is in one sense made up of the divided remnants of the nationalist, or Kuomintang, force led by wartime Generalissimo Chang Kai-Shek, who fled to the island after defeat. On the other hand, Okinawan citizens often have close familial lineage with their ancestors from mainland China.[31] This means that they regularly conduct pilgrimages to family graves and other sites of religious and cultural importance on the continent.[32] Such legacies, therefore, provide a further deeply rooted, foundational layer of integration in terms of promoting the islands as a hub through which to restructure and redirect regional trade relations from a point of relative neutrality. This combination of centuries-old historical legitimacy, harking back to Ryukyu tribute missions paid to imperial China, and proactive engagement with China's contemporary economic rise, has clearly raised alarm bells in Washington and Tokyo (Dasgupta 2023). In these centres of power, conservative actors have sought to seize upon and depict Governor Tamaki's efforts as undermining the US–Japan

31 The nature of these links are discussed in Ryukyu-history.com (2017).

32 As explained in interviews with residents of Itoman City (31 January 2023) and Nago City (12 July 2023).

alliance's security over the Southwest Islands, which they are attempting to fortify. Hence, rather than embracing Okinawa's initiative as a welcome means by which to spur economic growth in rural Japan and stabilize regional relations, it is depicted by centre-right-leaning politicians and press media as kowtowing to China. Therein, Beijing is cast as seeking any advantage possible to infiltrate weakness around Japan's luminal maritime perimeters of the extended First Island Chain (see Japan Forward 2023).

As explicated further in Chapter 4, this kind of interpretation lends itself to the escalation of tensions and the creation of a regional arms race (O'Hanlon 2022). In the process, American and Japanese authorities seek to strengthen military fortifications, demonize the regime in Beijing and isolate Okinawan Prefectural authorities to prevent them from deepening engagement with China (Davis 2023). A further reason for such conservative tactics on the part of Tokyo and Washington stems from the perceived limits on economic value that can be extracted at national and transnational corporate levels in terms of the trade and tourism-based activities being explored by Governor Tamaki and his regional interlocutors.[33] This again is where the comparison with Taiwan becomes relevant. One of the means by which Taipei is able to enjoy a burgeoning trade relationship with mainland China beyond transit and tourism, while also gaining a form of security guarantee from Washington (although this is strategically ambiguous), is through its specialization in indispensable technologies. Semiconductor design and production is the most obvious of these. Taiwan's capture of a huge portion of this vital market means that in effect what is, on the face of it, an economic asset has also become central to guaranteeing the island's sovereignty because of its importance to all sides, including China, the US and Japan (The Economist 2023). The last two states certainly could not idly sit by and allow the PRC to capture all of Taiwan's semiconductor design centres and other vital infrastructure through a unilateral invasion and forced reassimilation, as these are also essential to their own economies. In addition, and more extensively than Okinawa is able or willing to develop, Taipei is also seeking to diversify its cutting-edge

33 For critique of the Prefectural Government's plans in this regard, see Sumida & Tritten (2011).

technologies to increase the sustainability of this deterrence mechanism (Chang 2023).

Though growing in regional influence and economic potential for China, the same mechanism cannot currently be observed on Okinawa's outlying islands. Conversely, however, the inhabited islands of Miyakojima, Ishigaki and Yonaguni have sufficiently valuable strategic assets for Japan to defend them in earnest if China moved to invade any or all of them (see Ryall 2020). At present, although a seemingly remote possibility, recent military fortifications and escalations, as discussed further in Chapter 4, mean that the fragile status quo is shifting towards an increased likelihood of conflict, or at least confrontation, over these outposts (Japan MOD 2023). While the outcome of any such aggression initiated by China would probably be negative from a Chinese point of view, given their relative estimated military capabilities, the vulnerability of these islands, all of which lie closer to mainland Asia than Tokyo, is clear. The potential of future attacks or incursions has, therefore, not been lost on key actors hailing from their respective locales. Miyakojima is a case in point. Here leading officials, such as Mayor Zakimi and potential mayoral candidates, have set out a vision for realizing the diversification of the island that includes both economic and military aspects.[34] In other words, while continuing to fortify the island robustly, they argue, the existing reliance upon tourism (mostly from mainland China) can be diversified to include the development of a higher education sector and green energy industry among other projects. This proposes the possible use of disused government buildings to construct an island-wide international university campus, in addition to harnessing the massive potential for leveraging sea power through solar, wind and hydrogen energy technologies.[35]

34 Explained during an interview with Mayor Kazuyuki Zakimi, Miyakojima City Office, 14 April 2023.

35 Explained during an interview with prospective mayoral candidate and entrepreneur Daisuke Nagahama, Miyakojima Wafutei, 15 April 2023.

CONCLUSION

This chapter has illustrated the key role that economics plays in situating Okinawa as a flashpoint. In so doing, it has also illuminated some of the means by which economic initiatives offer potential pathways towards the alleviation or mitigation of current tensions and disputes. Concretely, Okinawan Prefectural authorities have been identified as credible intermediators who are in a position to build on current regionally based efforts. These seek to deepen trade and exchange relationships as a means to further stabilizing the ECS rim. This builds confidence and reduces hostility between China and Japan in particular, with Okinawa's off-islands acting as a stark example of how this can be the case. Unfortunately, these cases, including confrontation over the Senkaku Islands, also illuminate how national government agendas are superseding these localized efforts. Furthermore, it has historically been economic incentives that have driven claims from China over the area and also now empower Beijing to push harder in pursuit of those vested interests as their relative strength vis-à-vis the US–Japan alliance grows. Nonetheless, at the same time there are still opportunities for Japan to encourage and welcome joint exploration and exploitation of this rich maritime zone. These include multiple formats along the lines that the Okinawan Prefectural Government has proposed through its basic plans and *21st Century Vision* document.[36] In addition, in an era of great and growing concerns over climatic change and marine pollution, the coupling of economic issues to environmental ones may be crucial in terms of developing a sustainable and diverse political economy. The realization of such a framework at the regional level might then promote integrated green tourism, scientific research and international sporting activities, among a host of industries that will rely heavily upon China and other neighbouring states' willingness to engage positively with Okinawa's commercial efforts and rejuvenated historical identity.

Much can be learned from the comparison with Taiwan in these regards. After all, Okinawa has considerable socio-cultural and, through its former trade hub and centuries-old tribute relations with mainland

36 Efforts by Okinawa Prefectural Governor Tamaki Denny to expedite this process are covered in Nippon Keizai Shimbun (2023).

Asia, economic legitimacy when it comes to deepening ties with Asian states. Indeed, these qualities both complement and, in some respects, arguably exceed those commanded by the contemporary ruling administration in Taipei. At the same time, however, Naha lacks any real legislative, judicial or administrative power of autonomy in its governance structures. This includes the prefecture's hosting of numerous military assets that, despite dwindling economic benefit, are likely to be defended at all costs in the name of national interests by Tokyo and Washington through the US–Japan alliance structure. The deficit of self-determination in these regards is especially acute when compared to Taiwan's ability to develop a world-leading role in the semiconductor industry while maintaining a substantive military deterrent *and* a de facto US security umbrella. Nevertheless, with growing awareness of these dynamics, and possessing a strong local identity akin to their Taiwanese neighbours, actors on both Okinawa's main and outlying islands are beginning to strategize as to how economic diversification might be coupled with military fortification in order to minimize vulnerability and maximize opportunities for growth. This thereby aims to utilize hard-power defence guarantees as well as developing economic assets, rather than framing security and economy as two sides of a (false) dichotomy, one of which must be chosen. In addressing the limitations of this approach, Chapter 4 zooms out from the subnational sphere. In contrast, it interrogates how such developmental planning, however well-intentioned and logically based on economic grounds, may prove insufficient to prevent geomilitary conflict. This concern becomes particularly grave when placed in the context of Okinawa's pivotal positionality as a flashpoint amid the turbulent international geopolitics that encircle the ECS and its surrounding maritime domain.

4

Okinawa as an international flashpoint

In this chapter I address the intersection of geostrategic security and politico-economic interests in the region by re-examining Okinawa as the "keystone of the Pacific" and what this role means. More specifically, in the context of the contemporary US-led Indo-Pacific security architecture, the discussion explains the strategic significance of Okinawa to the US–Japan alliance and how it is increasingly playing host to the intensified interoperability of American and Japanese forces throughout the Southwest Island Chain. This includes an assessment of new JSDF facilities on Okinawa as well as the security status quo of the Senkaku Islands. It concludes with the most likely projections for how the tense situation might be escalated or deescalated, as well as how these relate to tensions over the South China Sea and Taiwan Straits, as China continues to increase its security capabilities. In short, the chapter argues that unless significant changes are made or occur, Okinawa is highly likely to become a regional flashpoint. In this regard, it reflects the broader theme of the book in illustrating how a set of complex variables intersecting the state, market and society of the prefecture are inextricably linked to surrounding great power rivalries. Moreover, an examination of the available evidence suggests that these relationships are unstable, making conflict all the more likely as the centre of power transitions from the US and its allies towards China.

In contrast, however, even when these structural dynamics constrain the range of possible policy actions, which in this case appear to be pushing Okinawa towards being a focal point for military action, cooperative security initiatives aimed at averting direct military conflict may be possible. In that regard, the argument is made that these need to be informed by credible ideational concepts that contain sufficient mutual compatibility between a range of stakeholders. In order to evidence the above, a number of leading IR theories are simplified and applied to the Okinawan case study. This involves summarizing their key ideas, recapitulating how they are used to understand unfolding situations on the ground and sea, and combining their most pertinent insights to gain a clearer picture. By doing so, I unpack the state and non-state drivers of structural power, explain how these result in specific forms of policy-making and illustrate the key ideational elements that inform those policy-makers' decision-making. Thereby the complexity and importance of Okinawa, as the so-called keystone of the Pacific, is revealed in terms of its potential as a focus point from which to – in contrast to its framing as a flashpoint – positively shape the future of regional security.[1]

STRUCTURAL TENSIONS: OKINAWA AT THE INTERSECTION OF US–CHINA–JAPAN–TAIWAN RELATIONS

It bears repeating that Okinawa amounts to only 0.6 per cent of Japan's total landmass yet sits at the fulcrum of great power rivalries between the ECS and the Pacific Ocean (Mason 2023: 117). In material terms, this geostrategic importance is evidenced by its fortification, with multiple US bases on the main island and major JSDF facilities on remote off-islands, including those already pointed to on Ishigaki Island, which has jurisdiction over the disputed Senkaku Islands, Miyako Island (where counter-strike missiles targeting China are set to be deployed) and Yonaguni Island, which is within physical sight of Taiwan. In fact, JSDF bases have grown by nearly five times the area of Okinawan land that they covered at the time of reversion to Japanese rule in 1972 (see Asahi Shimbun 2023b). This is all the more striking given the considerable resistance to equivalent US facilities and the push to reduce their scope and number. American installations include: key facilities at Kadena Air Base; MCAS Futenma, already identified as "the world's most dangerous base" for its location in the middle of Ginowan City;

1 For discussion of how Kadena Airbase on Okinawa Main Island, in particular, became the keystone of the Pacific in geostrategic terms, see Hong (2020).

and the controversial new facility being constructed as MCAS Futenma's proposed replacement, extending into the surrounding coral-filled bays from Camp Schwab at Henoko (Mitoma 2014: 20). The above are in addition to other new JSDF facilities that, in close cooperation with the US military, have been established throughout the Ryukyu Islands chain in a bid to shore up the US–Japan alliance's current hegemony over the ECS and western Pacific.[2] The central geographical position and advanced economic and infrastructural development on Okinawa, which is home to over a million residents, have thereby effectively transformed the archipelago into a physical barrier. This amounts to a maritime "great wall" (Son & Mason 2013); a fortification constructed by the combined militaries of the US and Japan against the perceived threat of China's maritime expansion to the east into the extended Indo-Pacific. Correspondingly, the standoff between these two camps creates what is typically referred to as a structural balance of power (see Nakatsuji 2023b).

However, the proximity of Taiwan to Okinawa's most westerly inhabited islands (Yonaguni Island, the Yaeyama Islands and Sakishima Islands) complicates the dynamics of competing regional geostrategies.[3] As it stands, the economic exclusion zone (EEZ) extending from Okinawa's islands forms the legal and tactical defence perimeter defended by the US–Japan Security Alliance. It also overlaps with China's interpretation when incorporating Taiwan, as well as with a separately designated ADIZ, which was unilaterally demarcated by Beijing in 2013. To complicate matters further, this includes the skies above the disputed Senkaku Islands. In addition, mainland Chinese and Taiwanese authorities both independently claim the entire waters surrounding the Senkakus and seek to apply their respective domestic laws to the area accordingly (Kawamura 2014: 27).

Against this backdrop, according to what IR scholars define as *realist* logic, a rising great power such as China will attempt to attain regional hegemony by challenging the existing hegemon: here the US. After

2 The argument is confirmed by recent local news media reports, such as Okinawa Times (2023a).

3 Further commentary is provided by Kyoto Hatakeyama, as per his 31 January 2023 address; see Hatakeyama (2023).

comprehensive victories in the Pacific War and Cold War – although weakened in the post-pandemic era – the US retains hegemonic control over the western Pacific (Zhou 2021). China is, therefore, now seeking to challenge that hegemony. The US projects its power westwards towards the Chinese mainland from the First Island Chain, with Okinawa Main Island acting as the "keystone" within that (Nakamura 2021: 1). As Beijing challenges this status quo, IR realism tells us that the structural imbalance caused by rising powers usually has disastrous consequences in terms of increasing the chances of confrontation. In other words, it usually leads to the outbreak of major military conflict (Abbasi 2020: 57; see also Allison 2019). Furthermore, intervening variables in the form of powers such as Japan, South Korea and Taiwan – to varying extents allied and integrated with the US hegemon and its security forces – further complicate this struggle for hegemonic dominance.

This is because the transition of power puts what realists refer to in structural terms as "hegemonic stability" – where one state suppresses would-be challengers and stakeholders by retaining overwhelming dominion – under a degree of stress. In the case of the waters surrounding Okinawa, such increased dynamism looks set to alter the balance of power across the ECS. US-led hegemonic stability is already being challenged by China's relative gains in terms of geomilitary expansion and unilateral alteration to the status quo. These have been made concrete (literally!) by the construction of maritime bases in adjacent regions, such as those in the South China Sea (SCS), relentless diplomatic pressure exerted on smaller regional states and military posturing towards, and cyber-attacks against, Taiwan (see Blanchard & Woo 2023). There is also evidence of Beijing escalating actions in the maritime theatre around the Okinawan islands between the ECS and Pacific Ocean (MOFA 2023). This is, therefore, behaviour consistent with the alarmingly conflict-prone realist predictions of a rising great power challenging the established hegemonic stability.

As a consequence, the US has sought to push back by reaffirming its commitment to defend Taiwan, strengthening interoperability with South Korea and focusing its increasingly interoperable military alliance with Japan on fortification of the First Island Chain (see Map 3, p.10), with a particular emphasis on supporting the establishment of the new JSDF facilities on Okinawa's islands (Gould 2023). For now, these fortification and alliance consolidation efforts offer the US a means by which to maintain a combined regional force capable of containing China. This temporarily sustains its hegemony while also extending the time frame for which it can expect containment to be effective through co-opting its alliance partners to shoulder a degree of both the economic costs and (potential) direct military losses incurred as the result of a war-fighting contingency. At the same time, from their perspective, Japan, South Korea and Taiwan are, by joining – or bandwagoning – with the US, creating an aggregate capability that can offset China's.

However, notwithstanding the above, at current rates of change such moves will ultimately not be sufficient to prevent China reaching a position of power-projection parity.[4] If this point is reached without major direct conflict, a more robust balance of power could theoretically be established, with neither side being sufficiently powerful to risk attacking the other directly for fear of mutually assured destruction. Nevertheless, because of further intervening variables, such as the domestic socio-economic changes documented in the preceding chapters, individual leadership decisions, shock events and intervention from non-state actors, a somewhat more nuanced understanding may be needed. These aspects can be assessed through what is usually referred to as neoclassical realism. Simply put, other actors and factors intervene so that the desired stable balance of power is unlikely to be reached peacefully (Uren 2020). In East Asia, from the shipping choke points of the SCS that carry 80 per cent of global trade, through the tense Taiwan Strait, to the rich fishing grounds and disputed territorial waters of the ECS, there are numerous catalysts that might trigger a localized conflict that leads to escalation. These could be instigated by subtle differences in leadership style or a misunderstanding (Foulon 2015: 636). For example, in the waters surrounding Okinawa, a bold move by a Chinese, Japanese or Taiwanese commander to intercept coastguard patrols or commercial vessels, an attempt by a high-profile politician to garner domestic political support through assertive foreign policy, or an accidental collision on the high seas, could act as the trigger. In these contexts, the two key elements of deterrence and reassurance become critical to whether conflict can be averted or not. Effective

4 For evaluation, see RAND (2020) and Foreign Relations Committee (2023).

deterrence, however, depends – paradoxically – primarily on the (re) establishment of a balance of power, which is problematic if the intervention was itself caused as a function of complex imbalances leading to escalation. Attempts at de-escalation through reassurance under these circumstances, therefore, become paramount.

The key point here is that deterrence, premised on a structural balance of power, remains vulnerable to these kinds of escalation scenarios triggered by incidents and accidents occurring around Okinawa (Hook, Mason & O'Shea 2015: 159). What is more, even without a dramatic or obvious catalyst event, deterrence's underlying vulnerability endures because of what is already an escalating security dilemma emanating from the ECS rim. This is taking the form of a great power arms race between the US (and to a certain extent Japan) and China. For instance, in addition to fortification, the GoJ's 2015 *anpo kanren hōan* legislation, or "war bill", was used to circumvent Article 9 (the so-called peace clause that prohibits the use of force for conflict resolution) of Japan's antimilitarist constitution through the reinterpretation and legalization of collective defence and counter-strike capabilities. These are evidently designed to cope with the rapidly changing ECS theatre and target Chinese technological advances (see Hasebe 2015). Furthermore, Tokyo has now transformed this law into policy by deploying 400 rockets on Okinawa's off-islands (on the Sakishima and Yaeyama island clusters) that can reach mainland China, with prospective changes also set to facilitate the stationing of such weaponry as far as Yonaguni Island, the most southwesterly point in the Japanese section of the First Island Chain (see Ryukyu Asahi 2023). There is considerable mission creep here, even though these weapons are currently deployed only on the key sites of Miyakojima Island and Ishigaki Island, albeit still several hundred kilometres to the west of Okinawa's main island. The suggestion is that it is only a matter of time before Yonaguni Island is also converted from its current status as a reconnaissance and observation base into a fortified military asset that can host combined US and JSDF forces.

These developments have been combined with overt demonstrations of American and Japanese political willingness – and indeed enthusiasm – to "seamlessly" integrate their military command, information sharing and logistical operations. All such changes serve to further fortify the First Island Chain with JSDF or joint-use bases and pull back key US military assets to the Second Island Chain, encompassing Guam, the Mariana Islands and Palau. These adaptations thereby counter Beijing's increasing ability to strike all targets stationed on the Ryukyu Islands (Midford 2024: 44). Meanwhile, China has countered these measures with "grey-zone" tactics. These not only include provisions to strike Okinawa and elsewhere along the First Island Chain but also involve constant attacks on Taiwan's digital and cyber infrastructure, as well as regularly entering the waters around the Senkaku Islands with "non-military" vessels, converting naval vessels into coastguard ships in the same area and legalizing the use of lethal force against any Japanese "incursions" (Ahmed 2022; Mason & Park 2024).

Therefore, from the perspective of these rapidly unfolding changes in the region, it will probably take more than the wise leadership often advocated by more optimistic realists to diffuse and deescalate the contemporary security environment surrounding Okinawa (He 2017). This is where a second IR theory can be utilized to address the core issues productively. We will call this the *liberal* layer of analysis. In contrast with IR realism, *liberalism*, broadly speaking, focuses more on a cooperative, win–win approach, and so allows us to address the complex distribution of interests operating in and around Okinawa more constructively. This includes within the constraints of the state-based material power structures identified above. Through the liberal lens these can be addressed most effectively via a nuanced understanding of the combined actions, or *agency*, of state leaders, myriad transnational economic actors and (to an extent) intersocietal relations.

FOREIGN POLICIES: SOURCE OF INSECURITY OR OPPORTUNITY TO EXERCISE WIN–WIN AGENCY?

Having, then, identified fragility in the balance of power, a process of more persuasive reassurance signalled by appropriate agency becomes central to militating against the escalating security dilemma unfolding from Okinawa across the ECS.[5] This does not mean that the various

5 Based on observations summarized from an interview with eminent historian of Japan's international relations, Sherzod Muminov, 19 March 2023.

key actors involved are inevitably beholden to the international structures of power that they are embedded within. It simply means that if foreign policies that avoid turning Okinawa into a flashpoint are to be formulated and implemented effectively, then these nation state-based aspects cannot be ignored when seeking to establish lasting regional security. Let us clarify, then, the distinction between combined, competing and complementary approaches that might aid us in achieving such goals. The combined, common-sense application of IR theories is essential to using such theory effectively in a way that allows liberal policies to build upon, rather than contradict, the realist logics outlined above. Put differently, there is often a misconception that states will either adopt an essentially realist *or* liberal approach to policy-making, when in reality nation states, statelets (such as Taiwan) and non-state actors (e.g. substates such as Okinawa) mostly undertake what can be described as liberal practices that operate on a foundation of realist, or *realpolitik*, understandings (Ikenberry 2009). In Okinawa's case, and throughout the wider ECS rim region, this involves engaging in trade, commerce and other forms of exchange while operating within the structural constraints dictated by the current status quo. Transnational actors, such as transnational corporations, international organizations and non-governmental organizations (NGOs) – also constrained but not enslaved by structural power – facilitate a significant proportion of these practices. Moreover, they do so without contradicting the essentially realist logics followed by national governments (Patalano 2014). This makes these kinds of actors and the agency they exercise potentially the key, or at least pivotal, to preventing Okinawa becoming a flashpoint in military terms.

Once agency is brought to the fore in this way, economic, societal and cultural aspects can take centre stage in the policy-making process. Furthermore, it is typically socio-economic interests manifest in state–non-state interactions that encourage corresponding reassurance measures to be developed, as evidenced in the example of substate initiatives focusing on regional diplomacy driven from Okinawa by the prefectural authorities and their affiliates.[6] Nevertheless, although each

6 Confirmed in an interview with *Okinawa Times* correspondent Akinori Ono, 30 March 2023, *Okinawa Times* head office, Naha.

of these actors has an ability to project and promote conflict avoidance and dispute resolution measures individually, there are still several areas where state-based actors remain of particular importance in this regard. At the leadership level, this includes at least the four central prongs, as put forward by theorist Janice Gross-Stein, which can be applied fruitfully to the Okinawa case study (Gross-Stein 1991: 431–51). They are as follows: minimizing or reducing activities that are likely to pressure an opponent or adversary into engaging in conflict; removing ambiguity over responses to escalatory incidents and accidents; establishing irrevocable or tangible commitments to specific kinds of behaviour; and developing regimes and systems that deliberately build confidence, reduce uncertainty and facilitate the growth and expansion of commercial and social exchanges.

Let us examine each in turn. First, with regard to avoiding direct conflict over the Senkaku Islands, for all their bellicose rhetoric and sabre rattling, Japan, the US, China and Taiwan have been remarkably successful in minimizing and reducing activities that might trigger some form of direct military or other deadly confrontation.[7] In addition to documented testimonies from Japanese officials and coastguard officers that evidence this as a deliberate strategy, the significance of such a strategy can be readily demonstrated through a comparison of activities that took place in the early part of the 2010s with those that took place afterwards in the surrounding waters of the ECS (Watanabe & Ono 2023). For example, the high-profile arrest of a Chinese fishing vessel's captain following its 2010 collision with a JCG patrol ship, which was ultimately authorized by then Prime Minister Naoto Kan, as well as the nationalization of the Senkaku Islands by Kan's successor, Yoshihiko Noda, both led to a dramatic escalation of tensions and tit-for-tat measures by Tokyo and Beijing (see Reuters 2010). These actions appeared to be geared primarily towards domestic audiences, stoking nationalist

7 For example, though rarely given public coverage, according to Okinawan Prefectural officials four specific measures were agreed upon between Chinese and Japanese coastguards and local authorities following the 2010 coastguard–fishing boat collision incident to increase communication and reduce the risk of accidental escalation (interview, Okinawa Prefectural Government, Naha, 15 March 2023).

sentiments in both China and Japan and leading to the Chinese military creating a new ADIZ that includes the airspace above the Senkakus in 2013 (Hirano 2014: 263). There has been a thin line between reassurance and escalation ever since, as Asia's two largest economies beef up their relative coastguard capabilities and vigorously patrol sovereign and bordering maritime zones, but they have not engaged militarily thanks to their mutual interests and an enhanced communications mechanism.[8] The JCG also relies on information supplied by US and Japanese militaries, while emphasizing their non-military role and deliberately avoiding physical challenges to China's coastguard ships operating in the area beyond the level of verbal warnings and requests to withdraw from Japanese sovereign territory.[9] Japan's commercial airlines also circumvent China's unilaterally declared ADIZ.

Second, in terms of removing ambiguity, the challenge is becoming increasingly severe despite various positive de-escalation measures. Specifically, security is threatened by the developing situation in neighbouring waters, such as the Taiwan Strait (Nakatsuji 2023a: 140). This includes the escalation of military posturing during the early twenty-first century by Beijing and senior US leaders' seemingly contradictory assertions regarding US resolve to defend Taipei should China move to invade it, including those made by President Joe Biden as America's Commander in Chief. Walk-back statements from Whitehouse staff and visits by high-profile US politicians to Taiwan also increase perceived uncertainty. Such actions have, therefore, significantly increased ambiguity in the region (see Hagstrom 2022; Brunnstrom & Hunnicutt 2022). Similarly, as a key US alliance partner, the GoJ has been forced to fudge its responses to unclear American Presidential statements and speak in vague language to avoid further muddying the water, while at the same time Japanese politicians have been outspoken in both their support for, and opposition to, US policies, respectively (see, e.g., Aso 2023). Tokyo's governing authorities are also concerned that as part of

8 A new mechanism was launched in 2018; see Kyodo News (2018).

9 It is worth noting that the majority of "incursions" by Chinese vessels that are reported in popular media are actually entering into the bordering maritime zone (*setsuzoku suiiki*) rather than violating Japan's actual sovereign waters (Okinawa Prefectural Government 2021).

any Chinese invasion of Taiwan, China might feel it necessary to nullify or blockade the maritime zone surrounding Taipei. This would probably include Okinawa's Yonaguni Island. Hence, clarification on the circumstances under which Japan would view a contingency in the Taiwan Strait as an existential threat to its own national security – thereby legitimizing mobilization of the JSDF for military defence – is one means by which reassurance over ambiguities might be strengthened in this regard.[10]

Third, in terms of establishing irrevocable or tangible commitments to specific kinds of behaviour, Beijing has been clear that any declaration of independence by Taipei, or overt recognition of Taiwan's sovereignty by the US, would be red lines that would spark an immediate military response (Tan 2023). In other words, Beijing claims that it would legitimate, and indeed oblige, China to mobilize the PLAN to reunify Taiwan Island with the mainland by force. At the same time, state authorities and business communities in the US and Japan have striven to impress upon the CCP's leadership that a violent, unilateral alteration of the status quo would result in a swift and decisive response that would be damaging for the PRC. In addition, since Biden's predecessor, Donald Trump, took office, official American statements regarding the defence of Taiwan, although increasingly inconsistent, have shifted in tone to a position where the use of military force in tandem with regional allies has been conveyed as the expected response. This sends a clear message to China that any unprovoked attack will not be tolerated.

These same basic principles hold for the Senkaku Islands, where successive US presidents since George W. Bush have confirmed that the islands are covered by Article 5 of the US–Japan Security Treaty (Manyin 2016). This makes an attack on the islets an attack on the alliance. Yet Washington's unwillingness to be explicit about the islands' "sovereignty" per se offers fertile ground for Chinese authorities and militia to exploit as a justification for their attempts to dominate the surrounding waters on grounds of sovereign security, including inside Japan's EEZ. So far, these Chinese actors have stopped short of a physical landing on

10 The need for a clear independent security framework expressed by the GoJ was confirmed by Miyako Island Mayor Kazuyuki Zakimi (interview, Miyakojima City Office, 13 April 2023).

any of the Senkaku Islands, but they have by no means committed to not doing so in the future. In this regard, US indifference and avoidance of the recognition of sovereignty, combined with Japan's unwillingness to properly defend bordering waters around the ECS (rather than only Japanese islands located within them), creates further uncertainty. This makes these ECS maritime sites close to Okinawa a theatre where a more tangible and robust commitment by representatives of the US–Japan Security Alliance in response to increasingly assertive Chinese incursions may come to be viewed as a necessity over time.[11]

Finally, by way of confidence-building measures, it is evident that the economy will play a key role if the growth and expansion of commercial and social exchanges over the ECS between China, Japan, the US and Taiwan are to flourish. Considerable progress has already been made in this area. For example, Chinese investment in Okinawan land and the booming post-pandemic international tourism industry, in addition to collaborative university-based scientific research undertaken within the prefecture, are sectors that present burgeoning trade and exchange opportunities. They also offer the potential for sustained economic growth.[12] These initiatives are based on what might be referred to as mercantilist practices of maximizing profit and financial incentive with increasingly deregulated and decentred international business regulations. For them to act as a reassurance mechanism, however, initiatives obviously need to be linked either implicitly or explicitly to the issue of maintaining a lasting peace over the ECS (Tanji & Broudy 2017: 77). Specifically, discursive and legal reassurances from political actors on all sides are typically required to underwrite and enhance investor confidence and confirm that there is a substantial economic incentive for maintaining peace and avoiding conflict around Okinawa (Mason 2023: 129). This also requires the strategic promotion of socio-economic

11 At the same time, local authorities, including the JCG and Okinawa Prefectural Government, continue to press for demilitarized responses to China, see *Okinawa Times* (2023b).

12 An extensive plan of how this might be achieved on Miyako Island to incorporate higher education, multiple industries and governmental sectors was provided by prospective mayoral candidate Daisuke Nagahama in a 12 April 2023 interview with the author.

interests without stoking exclusionary nationalism. As such, a conceptual, liberal shift in thinking is needed, whereby normative considerations that coalesce around a set of shared ideological principles at the elite level become pivotal. To address the mechanisms by which these can be realized, we turn to *constructivism* as a further IR prism that offers insight into how changes in ideas can result in changes on the ground or across the sea. Having thus far delineated underlying structural power and the individual and collective exercising of complex agency from positions of self-interest within it, (social) constructivism offers an ideas-based lens through which to view revised versions of realist logic and inform liberal understandings of practical foreign policy formation.

THE POWER OF IDEAS: FROM FLASHPOINT TO CONFLUENCE OF COMMERCIAL INTERESTS

Continuing her decades-long protest against US military bases, one veteran Okinawan campaigner told me that the priority for the security of the ECS region should be to rediscover and strengthen historical identities among island nations. This, she continued, would involve reducing American military facilities and having the GoJ take full responsibility for its current role in perpetuating Okinawa's plight, as well as for its past colonial aggressions.[13] The scope of this statement highlights the current lack of mutual empathy and communication between the various perceived adversaries around the ECS rim, in both material and conceptual terms. It also illustrates how these aspects would evidently need to be substantively increased for the kinds of constructive reassurance and atonement for historical errors put forward by my interlocutor to be realized. In response, a social constructivist approach holds that because the perceptions of others' intentions have a powerful tendency to dictate policy actions, the relative positionality of political and economic ideas and the identities they inform matter greatly. More specifically, in the case at hand, these become central to the process of

13 Interview with Takazato Suzuyo, 23 March 2023, Henoko, *gēto mae* (in front of the (Camp Schwab) gate).

forming alliances and adversaries. In essence, a deeper understanding of your friends and enemies helps to increase communication and reduce the risk of conflict, but this phenomenon has a far higher likelihood of averting combat if adversaries think in a similar way. By way of a positive example, with specific regard to Okinawa's security environment, changing perceptions and issue framings were central to the way in which Japan's ideological mainstream was transformed from accepting a dictatorship into expecting a modern, liberal, democratic state following the Pacific War. This transformation was realized from the starting point of an exclusionary nationalist authoritarian state immediately before and during the Second World War, which had led to discrimination towards those deemed not fully Japanese, including Okinawans, and colonialist expansion across the wider Indo-Pacific region (Takenaka 2014).

Ironically, despite being freed from Japan's imperial clutches under American assurances of liberty and democracy, Okinawa's population were once again forced to live as second-class citizens subjected to protracted military rule and racial discrimination until, and beyond, the time of reversion. Nevertheless, although there have been degrees of regression and remilitarization in the years since, Tokyo's leaders now espouse similar market-led economic ideas and societal values, enforced through legal and rules-based norms, to those of Japan's postwar ally, the US (Madison 2019: 125). In addition, and perhaps of even greater significance, is that regional states such as South Korea and statelets akin to Taiwan, albeit without a formal alliance in the latter case, also promote comparable foreign policy narratives informed by similar ideas. The result is a surprisingly broad diplomatic alignment that is maintained discursively but also reinforced through public rhetoric. This includes the popularly articulated narrative of being "like-minded" states, referring essentially to discourses about a "rules-based" order promulgated by executive elites, which are supposedly representative of their populations. Such discourses thereby help to establish mutually reinforcing identities that create an in-group in contrast to an out-group, or *other*, represented mostly in the case of tensions around Okinawa by China (Hagström & Gustafsson 2015).

Yet, based on the discursive content of those same supposedly rival elites, US–Japan security identity is not in polemic contrast with that adopted by the PRC and its rulers. Through a brief comparison of relevant Chinese, Taiwanese and Korean statements with those emanating from Tokyo and Washington, it becomes evident that despite contested histories and identities, specific rhetoric referring to how the ECS should be governed and operated within is strikingly similar across all parties and actors. Moreover, all those with skin in the ECS game promote the same kinds of normative development (MOFA 2008). Similarly, this is also espoused remarkably uniformly by Okinawa's multiparty elected Diet members. Aiko Shimajiri of the ruling LDP, for instance, despite advocating a strengthening of the US–Japan alliance and reinforcing the distinction between the groupings of like-minded states listed above, reassures us that: "The priority is for commercial and economic activities to be carried out smoothly and peacefully. The government is not in a position to designate specific countries as a threat, but assured transportation (safe passage for shipping and flights etc.) has to be an absolute prerequisite."[14]

As further illustrated below, all leading ECS stakeholders also express formal legal frameworks as the most practical means by which to achieve these almost universally posited priorities. Correspondingly, such prioritizations invariably identify with norms of commercial development, economic exchange and peaceful cooperation.

The formalized tenets for realizing such goals within the US–Japan alliance framework, through the promotion of the Free and Open Indo-Pacific concept (Hosoya 2019), for example, also align remarkably unproblematically with rhetoric from the alliance partners' mutually identified adversaries, which again in this case amounts essentially to CCP-led China. Beijing's leadership has repeatedly postulated the concept of a peaceful global order based on win–win (positive-sum) exchanges and a flourishing economy, realized primarily in East Asia through extensions of the Belt and Road Initiative, which China insists does not amount to an attempt to supplant the US and its allies in geomilitary terms.[15] In this regard, despite being unapologetic over incursions into the waters and skies around the Senkaku Islands, as

14 Aiko Shimajiri, interview, 14 March 2023, via email (author's translation).

15 It is important to distinguish between the ECS and other regions in this regard. For a counter-argument relating to China's claims regarding its broader geostrategic ambitions, see Blank (2019).

well as repeatedly intimidating Taiwan and traversing the maritime space between the outlying Ryukyu Islands with naval vessels, the PRC has not deviated substantively from its aspirations to realize the rules-based coexistence outlined above. Mouthpieces for the CCP such as the China Daily and China Global Television Network (CGTN), along with leading Chinese establishment academics, including the influential Yan Xuetong, have reinforced this position (Yan 2006: 5; see also, e.g., CGTN 2022). This suggests that conflict over Okinawa is not inevitable. Rather, achievement of mutually beneficial goals through constructive dialogue is conceivable if an effective framework for implementation can be agreed and the existing structural dynamics and constraints are candidly incorporated into any such process by all parties from the outset.

Concurrently, Taiwan and South Korea each lay separate, independent claims to parts of the ECS and identify with similar norms. These are embedded within their middle-power identities, which for the most part supersede contestation over formal recognition of the former and reunification of the latter. Both states have historical territorial disputes with Japan as well as a formal alliance and strategic alignment, respectively, with the US. They also both rely heavily on trade with China (Bureau of Foreign Trade of the Republic of China 2023; Trading Economics 2023). In addition, again somewhat ironically given the respective political and military alignments of the two entities, government statements from Taipei make an unequivocal claim to the Senkaku Islands based on essentially the same historical claims as those asserted by Beijing (Wang & Stamper 2014: 45). These rest on the dubiously constructed notion that the islets were only formally recognized as Japanese sovereign territory through Tokyo's imperialist 1895 Treaty of Shimonoseki after victory in the first Sino-Japanese War, in which Japan grabbed territories from a weakened and deceived Qing-ruled China, only to then relinquish them following the 1951 San Francisco Peace Treaty. In this sense, the obstacle to aligning mainland Chinese and Taiwanese claims is not manifest in separation from their respective identities. Nor does it rely only upon establishing a balance of power and specific reassurance actions to support it, but also on a willingness to agree upon their shared Chinese identity.

Identities are, of course, socially constructed. Hence the importance of shifting ideas relating to the respective identities attached to this dispute is all the more evident. This is further reinforced given that both sets of claims are essentially the same in claiming the Senkakus for one "China", so relying pivotally on what that concept means (Wang & Stamper 2014). Similarly, South Korea's stake in the ECS waters, although more significant in terms of regional dynamics as a whole and less relevant to the specifics of the Senkaku dispute, is based upon a historical conception and identity of Korea, incorporating both halves of the Korean Peninsula (Manicom 2014: 259). Hence, putting North Korea's China-aligned regime temporarily to one side, this is articulated by Seoul's state, business and media actors through narratives of historical victimhood at the hands of regional powers such as Japan. Notwithstanding, Koreans, like their regional counterparts, overwhelmingly support a more stable, productive and mutually beneficial status throughout the ECS, enforced through the rule of law (Becker-Weinberg 2020).

With some justification, Tokyo rejects the specific legal basis for each of these versions of history championed by its neighbouring countries, claiming, contrarily, that the Senkaku Islands were incorporated into Japan's sovereign territories as *terra nullius* prior to the initiation of the First Sino-Japanese War. Even so, the nature of the *terra nullius* status is somewhat arbitrary. Moreover, there are relatively limited resources accessible in, and beneath, the waters around the Senkaku Islands, which serves to minimize their intrinsic resource value, and they have a minimal presence in Japanese historical national identity construction. As such, it would seem plausible that Tokyo's lawmakers could reconfigure their framing of the Senkaku Islands' status and significance to align more publicly with the kind of win–win diplomatic rhetoric being projected by their adversaries in Beijing and local authorities on Okinawa towards aspirations for the region more broadly. For instance, bipartisan politicians have an opportunity to argue that diplomatic flexibility would gain Japan greater international prestige as a renewed leader of regional diplomacy (Hauken 2020). In other words, despite repeated recent assertions by leading Japanese political figures that the security environment along the First Island Chain is increasingly harsh – thereby expediting unprecedented increases in defence spending – rhetorical gymnastics might allow Japan to reposition or even reinvent itself in this regard. This would probably involve the promotion of an identity that prioritizes the kinds of liberal trade policies detailed above while still operating from a position of strength within the current regional power structures. These changes would then be further justified through a recalibration of how important the Okinawan islands and the wider ECS are to Japan's energy security and fishing industries, as part of a broader normative framework led by cooperative dialogue.

From this perspective, the only tangible barrier to achieving more convivial relations across the ECS is the interpretation of historically embedded national identities. In this respect, Okinawa, with its unique historical identity based on antimilitarism and trade among regional states – rather than accept a framing as the potential flashpoint for future conflict – might offer a site of relative neutrality and localized arbitration (Okinawa Prefectural Government 2023). Nevertheless, questions remain over whether such a role is possible given its formally subjugated administrative legal status as no more than a single prefecture of Japan. However, Okinawa's history as an independent trading kingdom, along with popularly cultivated narratives of peace and self-determination encapsulated in the prefecture's "all Okinawa" movement, allow the islands to identify as a credible mouthpiece for the promotion of more demilitarized means by which to achieve shared normative goals. In that sense, these Okinawan characteristics might contribute substantively towards circumventing what have become rigid and divisive regional great power rivalries. This approach has already been endorsed by China, as illustrated through President Xi Jinping's comments emphasizing historical amity between China's Fuzhou Province and the Ryukyu Kingdom (see Okinawa Times 2023c). Similarly, Prefectural Governor Tamaki Denny, like his predecessors, has been encouraged to make independent visits to the Chinese mainland, as part of regional initiatives led by Okinawa's prefectural authorities. These activities mirror countless Ryukyuan residents and wider family members who regularly return to the Asian mainland to pay respects to their ancestors as part of deeply rooted religious and cultural practices that are continued to this day on Okinawa.[16]

---

16 Unlike mainland Japan, Okinawa's primary (quasi-)religious practice is ancestor worship (*sosen sūhai*) rather than Buddhism or Shinto.

Despite this deep socio-cultural affinity, however, given the structural balance of power detailed at the outset of this chapter, it is not surprising that such rhetorical and diplomatic overtures directed at Okinawa by Beijing draw considerable suspicion from Washington and Tokyo. Instead of being welcomed as a sign of underlying empathy, they are viewed generally as a means of encroachment into Japanese sovereignty through a point of contested liminality, namely Okinawa.[17] Nevertheless, while Okinawans support a strong US–Japan alliance by a clear majority, they also oppose the disproportionate number of military bases stationed throughout their islands. This is due largely to perception. In other words, it amounts to believing that the US–Japan Security Treaty provides a sufficient degree of security with which to sustain the economy, society and socio-cultural identity of Okinawa Prefecture through extended deterrence. As already alluded to, however, that identity is contested both internally and externally. Either way, residents of the Ryukyu Islands would almost universally like to see increased trade and tourism with China, Taiwan and other regional states. In this regard, instead of suppressing and dividing Okinawan opinion and agency in a form that creates a reinforced impression of continued imperial imposition and colonization – as also experienced in past eras by China, Taiwan and Korea no less vis-à-vis Japan – the US and Japan might adopt alternative approaches. For example, these could include more convincingly and inclusively working with actors on Okinawa to develop a historically grounded and integrated identity that can lay claim to an inclusive, cooperative agenda in relation to all these states. There is certainly scope for something like this to combine current economic interests with the promotion or adaptation of new and existing regional institutional frameworks. Potentially, these would also explicitly address the balance of power either side of the First Island Chain. In so doing, Okinawa offers a site of convergence that contains mutually shared aspects of the historical identities present among each

17 The significance of how sovereignty at the margins in this case has become "reconstructed" in some sense outside of Westphalian framings has been emphasized in open discussion by leading experts in the field, as expressed by Ching-Chang Chen at his 9 June 2023 in-person event in Chatan Town, Okinawa.

ECS rim state and (semi-)autonomous entity. The question remains, though, as to whether it can play a significant role in efforts to refocus towards the expansion of bilateral and multilateral trade regimes and grassroots diplomacy, rather than acting as a locus for fortification and conflict.

CONCLUSION

In sum, the sections above have drawn upon and combined the underlying principles of IR realism, liberalism and constructivism in order to provide a nuanced analysis of why Okinawa is likely to once again become a keystone in the Pacific as a potential geopolitical flashpoint. It has also offered tentative lines of enquiry into how this might be avoided. The chapter has elucidated how there is a need to re-evaluate and pragmatically re-engage with the historically rooted tensions that surround Okinawa over the ECS. In that respect, the Ryukyu Islands chain has to be put into the current global context of major wars and conflict so as to fully appreciate its importance and gravity. Changes to the security postures of Japan, China, the US and Taiwan, among other regional states, are taking place against a background of ongoing and escalating warfare being waged around the world. It is in that sense that a discussion of the challenges relating to Okinawa is undertaken in part with the goal of contributing to greater relative regional security in East Asia, where tensions are also threatening to boil over. To that end, the above discussion of concrete examples contains the blueprint, or at least conceptual foundation, for how issues of lasting peace might be more constructively engaged with. This is fleshed out in greater detail and practicality through a further series of detailed scenarios, in the final chapter that follows, with reference to how political, economic and security-based aspects need to be more effectively integrated.

For now, in specific relation to security, it is worth re-emphasizing here that a credible, conceptually renewed analytical framework, underpinned by a condensed combination of IR theories, presents itself as a likely starting point from which to move forwards. Such an approach can be used to inform constructive, comprehensive policy innovations, incorporating underlying interests, a wide range of actors and the diverse ideas and identities that they are driven by. Moreover, this reworking of theories reminds us of how theory informs practice on the international stage, because, even when implicit within policy-making models, it is used in complex cases such as Okinawa to offer logical paths to greater cooperation and conflict mitigation. It also facilitates this without invoking religious or other emotive triggers that tend to obstruct pragmatism in this field, particularly in the historically charged context of East Asia. The kind of discourse-based evidence unpacked above, focusing on similarities, common ground and shared objectives, thereby shines a light on how truncated versions of theories such as realism, liberalism and constructivism are particularly useful in penetrating otherwise polemic or parochial political rhetoric. The current situation surrounding Okinawa is a clear example of this, because it indicates that if Okinawan agency can be amplified and leveraged via historical identity and accompanying rhetoric in the public sphere, perhaps even to the level of greater self-determination, subtle but important changes to more structural aspects of regional competition might be realized. This is particularly pertinent in the Okinawan case given its authenticity as the site of a peaceful regional trade hub and cultural integration through time. The islands, therefore, also have the potential to act as a mutually agreeable focus point, rather than as a flashpoint, from which surrounding great powers might initiate more cordial relations.

In other words, by working from a starting point of assumed competition for material power, and engaging with the key agents that seek to exercise control and influence, it is possible to reach a level of mutual empathy and complementarity of interests that incorporate distinct identities without resorting to war as the extension of politics by other means. In these respects, contrary to more pessimistic accounts, explanatory power is a weapon against conflict at flashpoints of great power rivalry. In the ECS security domain, it is clear from the evidence examined that polemic ideologies prevalent among the ECS states, as well as the perceived need of political actors to demonize external adversaries, does exacerbate the pursuit of shared goals such as regional peace and prosperity. Nonetheless, these negative aspects are largely based on cognitive illusions. This is the case even at the state level, where official policies – once stripped of inflammatory rhetoric – are strikingly well aligned in the majority of cases. They include the prioritization of averting kinetic military engagement, the creation of a stable political economy, a rules-based order and promotion of an optimal trading environment.

In the case at hand, the relevance of such an approach also needs to be contextualized by reinterpreting Japan's Cold War security policy in relation to the dispersed and locally diverse prefecture that is Okinawa. Largely as an extension of US foreign policy in Japan's case, this has contributed to the gradual shift in power-projection capabilities between the US and its allies vis-à-vis China, in favour of the latter. Tokyo's overbearing attitude towards Naha and its use of the Okinawan islands as a porn in their broader security strategy has also limited the relevance of intervening variables that emanate from Okinawa and its people. In that respect, the three core IR theories applied to the analysis above also help us to identify some of the key constraints preventing an improved security environment from being realized by cooperative actors across the region. These include the potential dangers caused by a rising great power, in this case China, as it challenges the US as the regional hegemon. However, having gained an understanding of the structural elements of geomilitary and economic power driving this process in realist terms, a more liberal perspective offered cause for optimism regarding the non-inevitability of great power conflict and opportunities for positive-sum gains. This conclusion is buttressed by the evidence of encouraging aspects resulting from a complexity of actors and interests on Okinawa. In metaphorical terms, we might claim here that more cooks do not spoil the Okinawan broth. Rather, they offer new flavours or lines of development, such as in marine sports, ecotourism, collaborative scientific exploration and private–public investment projects. These are incentivizing multiple state-based and non-state actors to affect a process of structural change via their pursuit of diverse individual interests. At the same time, they are greatly disincentivizing military conflict. Finally, socially constructed logics of ideational and normative change offer credible means by which to adjust policy-making towards facilitating these liberal initiatives through more constructive, empathetic dialogue in the pursuit of shared goals. These include the priorities already listed above and open a space to focus on historical and contemporary commonality, rather than resorting to a destructive process of polarized *othering*. This has specific implications not only for the public framing of competing territorial claims, including those pertaining to the Senkaku Islands, but also for broader regional relations, within which almost all states and relevant actors subscribe not only to similar guiding principles and priorities but also to comparable processes by which they should be implemented.

There is clearly some way to go before shared norms translate into cordial relations. However, when viewed through these combined IR prisms, Okinawa's powerful antimilitarist norms and history of independent regional trade emerge as a potential locus for developing policy initiatives drawing on the framework applied above. Okinawan identity is particularly significant in propelling such a process from within the prefecture because of both the legitimacy its unique history provides and the urgency of the current security challenges it faces. This includes being in the unenviable position of Japan's most heavily fortified prefecture amid a backdrop of escalating global conflict. As such, Chapter 5 concludes this volume by weighing the relative pros and cons, before putting forward a series of negative and positive scenarios that sketch pathways towards practical policy steps. In these regards, it draws on each of the spheres addressed thus far to advance a holistic argument for how Okinawa might maximize its chequered past and current status proactively. This includes adapting creatively and with flexibility to the present security environment and working towards playing a more central role in improving relations between ECS rim states and stakeholders.

5

Okinawa's fight for a flashpoint-free future

POLITICS, ECONOMICS AND SECURITY: NEGATIVE AND POSITIVE SCENARIOS

This book has argued that for political, economic and geostrategic reasons, Okinawa is in danger of becoming a flashpoint for great power conflict. This has been argued from the perspective of its turbulent history, as well as its precarious present and uncertain future. The prefecture's complex domestic politics and society, tensions between local and mainland economic vested interests – along with their impact upon fragile ecosystems – and the islands' challenging international geomilitary position all compound this designation as a probable convergence point for major interstate violence. In light of the evidence presented thus far, this final chapter brings together the key elements discussed above and sets out a series of plausible scenarios for each of their core spheres of interaction. The aim of this endeavour is to shine a light on the primary obstacles to progress as well as illuminating credible pathways to more positive outcomes in each case. Within this context, the most significant variables are consistently identified as leading state and non-state political actors, economic incentives and disincentives, and pivotal shifts in the broader international geostrategic landscape. After highlighting the depth and breadth of the challenge at hand in each case, an alternative scenario is then put forward as a form of recommendation for enabling dialogue towards the creation of mechanisms through which constructive change and policy innovation might be realized. This begins from the Okinawan perspective by sketching negative and positive scenarios that address the seemingly irreconcilable tensions between long-standing domestic political adversaries driving discord on the islands.

LONG-STANDING LOCALIZED RIVALRY: DANGERS OF DIVIDED RULE

We have duly highlighted the challenges posed by the complex nature of Okinawa's domestic politics and how this might contribute towards the islands becoming a flashpoint for more wide-reaching conflict. Similarly, in some of the more compelling negative analyses put forward by analysts and political actors, localized political divisions become a key factor in leading the prefecture, or at least certain municipalities within it, towards in-fighting and interparty discord that threatens the cohesion of any potential Okinawa-wide unity. The historical antecedents of contemporary political divisions within Okinawa Prefecture have also been discussed at some length (see Chapters 1 and 2). It bears repeating, then, given the implications for broader political battles waged from within the prefecture, that the challenge here is not simply a case of Okinawa versus Japan or the US. It includes long-running disagreements on both the main island itself and between Naha, the prefectural capital, and the outer off-island clusters, such as the Yaeyama and Sakishima groups. These remote outposts have experienced a very different contemporary history to that of their counterparts surrounding the seats of limited localized power on the Okinawan mainland. In some cases this disparity – including in relation to base hosting and external funding streams – continues to manifest itself in festering resentment at being controlled by a prefectural administrative hub that lies hundreds of miles from their shores.

Meanwhile, central authorities in Tokyo have consistently exploited and continue to exploit these divisions in what can only be described as a form of divide and rule politics. Though far from being the only impediment, this dynamic persistently undermines Naha's ability to galvanize meaningful support for greater autonomy and self-determination at a prefecture-wide level. Going forwards, such aspects of division and centralized governance may, therefore, prove critical to preventing grassroots opposition towards central authorities on the Japanese mainland. This includes towards what have become increasingly escalatory policies pursued by the ruling LDP-led GoJ in terms of its use of the prefecture in the international sphere as a bulwark against a rising China. In that regard, we have seen how Japan's ruling elite are in one sense overseeing a resurgence of the *suteishi*, or throwaway stone, scenario already experienced by Okinawa at the end of the Pacific War. Then, the IJA sought to slow the American advance up the First Island Chain on its counter-offensive towards mainland Japan by fortifying the Okinawan mainland. A third of Okinawa's population was sacrificed in the "typhoon of steel" that resulted. In the absence of more unified domestic politics that can rally to rein in escalatory dynamics unfolding across the ECS, could a comparable future invasion by the PRC be triggered and bring about a repeat of such horrors?

China's imminent conquest or invasion of outlying inhabited Japanese islands seems extremely unlikely at the time of writing. Nevertheless, recent events in Ukraine, Gaza, Myanmar and throughout sub-Saharan Africa and beyond demonstrate that conventional warfare remains a very real – and extremely deadly – extension of politics by other means. To this effect, Tokyo is undoubtedly seeking to keep Okinawa's people politically appeased, or at least tacitly compliant, and ensure that prefectural governors (effectively the most powerful office of local politicians) in particular wield highly limited power. This is partly so that the GoJ, in alliance with the US government, can fortify the islands with little or minimal local pushback. A striking example of this approach was demonstrated during then Chief Cabinet Secretary Yoshihide Suga's (later to become prime minister) 2015 visit to Okinawa. In the course of his stay, Suga sought to undermine then Prefectural Governor Takeshi Onaga's all Okinawa movement through the brazen use of divide and rule tactics implemented via the very visible exercising of so-called *ame to muchi* (candy and whip), or carrot and stick, measures that targeted local political figures.

"All Okinawa" was a political slogan used in an attempt to overcome subprefectural differences to unite behind preventing construction of the replacement base at Henoko. In response, Suga successfully undermined the move in the tradition of imperial Japan towards its colonial subjects, namely through incentivizing those willing to oppose the movement and threatening to penalize its leaders. The chief cabinet secretary visited municipalities within Okinawa one after the other, in effect offering economic incentives if they agreed to support the central government's proposals for construction of the new base and other military strengthening proposed in relation to outer island defence, in defiance of the popularly backed all Okinawa campaign. Governor Onaga was also, thereafter, penalized in real terms by the GoJ who reduced the *ikkatsu kōfukin*, or annual lump sum funding package, provided by Tokyo to Naha as a form of economic stimulus ostensibly designed to compensate the prefecture for hosting US military bases. The late Onaga and his successor, Tamaki Denny, were also subjected to concerted punitive legal suits by government ministries in which consecutive decisions taken by the Prefectural Government to block construction of the base at Henoko on environmental grounds were overruled and overturned through the law courts. Thereby, this case illustrates how the executive arm of government has effectively utilized its close relationship with the judiciary to prevent localized autonomy and self-determination. Moreover, as touched upon in Chapter 2, this occurs even where the Prefectural Government would, by the letter of the Constitution of Japan's Article 95, appear to have significant legitimacy in opposing government policy on grounds of having gained popular support.

In that respect, Okinawa's contested domestic politics is one of continued divide and rule prosecuted by central government, which is coupled with, and compounded by, disunity along ideological, generational and spatial fault lines among Okinawans. If these elements are not addressed through a more successful coupling of diverse local interests that can unite behind single issues, oppose entrenched vested interests and put forward compelling causes in a more consistent and coordinated form, Okinawan politics will probably remain little more than a talking shop for its dissatisfied citizens. In which case, it will continue to be acted out primarily for the benefit of parochial interests that compete for a limited ability to shape the prefecture's administrative status and future direction. At the same time, the already extensive influence of the ruling LDP will endure and perhaps be extended under the guise of collective national interest. This exploits the combination of local political discord and endemic apathy among younger voters towards promoting militarization while doing very little to prioritize the broader interests of Okinawa's people and its pristine natural environment.

Where such a centrally driven dynamic of GoJ authority prevails, then, rather than being necessary ingredients for a vibrant grassroots democracy within local government, the complexities of Okinawa's domestic politics become a counterproductive variable that tend to bring about immobilism and inertia. It has, thereby, remained a serious impediment in terms of realizing a meaningful divergence from the mostly conservative policy-making trajectories observed from the time of reversion to Japanese rule in 1972 to the present day. As a result of this disempowerment, the historically independent entity of the Ryukyus – now Okinawa Prefecture – is set to retain its unenviable position as the most likely of all Japan's major regions and municipalities to become a flashpoint for wider conflict. In response, local domestic politics will have little if any ability to prevent the serious negative consequences that may result from National Diet politicians and other leading officials actively encouraging escalation towards a faceoff with Asia's most powerful military: that commanded by the CCP. This trajectory is currently sustained as part of a ruling centre-right coalition. Their agenda is, thus, performatively reducing outlying Japanese territories, including Okinawa, to a function of increasingly robust rhetorical and practical demonstrations of territorial sovereignty, with general indifference towards public opinion or local politics.

"ALL OKINAWA" REVIVAL: POLITICAL VISION FOR PREFECTURE-WIDE UNITY

The projection of a positive scenario in response to the disempowerment of Okinawans outlined above, then, requires concerted political will at both local and national levels. One means by which to galvanize more effective prefecture-wide support in a coherent form might be through a renewed, and possibly rebranded, version of Onaga's "all Okinawa" concept. The original movement focused overwhelmingly on one specific issue, rather than the traditional ideological divide contested between Okinawa's progressive and conservative factions. Although mostly ineffective in terms of preventing base construction at Henoko, this supra-factional approach did gain some initial traction across the islands. The primary challenge, however, remains how to sustain its success in the face of mainstream media opposition or indifference, youth apathy and ignorance. The galvanization process itself should be relatively straightforward. After all, both conservatives and progressives, in their respective majority voices, opposed the base construction at Henoko to replace the ageing and unsafe facility at Futenma proposed by central government. This meant there was temporarily mass support within the prefecture for the united all Okinawa cause and Onaga was able to leverage considerable influence as prefectural governor to delay the project, despite both US and GoJ backing for it. Nonetheless, problems arise at the domestic level when the urgency of specific single issues changes or the dynamics driving the dispute shift. In that regard, Japan's central government and their American backers have been able to wait it out and slowly undermine the prefectural authorities by both encroaching on their political power base through financial support for rival candidates throughout the prefecture and directly targeting successive governors who oppose them by tying them up with legal disputes that become mired in Japan's glacially protracted court procedures. As such, a more robust framework for localized political unity is also required if centralized government policy is to be more constructively engaged with and effectively countered by Okinawans.

As part of such a move, an equivalent of the all Okinawa concept could be attached to a more diverse set of policy issues that include, but are not limited to, the disproportionate number of military bases on the island. In this regard, although many Okinawans are certainly concerned about the dangers of overmilitarization, particularly when it comes to US forces over whom they have almost no control, they are motivated primarily by the economic and social issues that directly impact their day-to-day lives. In other words, the downscaling of bases could be combined with a set of key policies in each of the most pertinent sectors that offer short- to mid-term benefits for a majority of Okinawans. This would apply whether they are on the main island or remote off-islands. The specific prospective economic elements are discussed in further detail in the sections that follow, but in terms of political causes, these could include: a percentage-based prioritization for Okinawan companies and subcontractors in relation to mainland enterprises as a means to provide local businesses with a comparative advantage and stimulate the real economy; development of more direct trade, tourism and exchange links with friendly regional states (or equivalent entities) such as South Korea, the Philippines, Indonesia,

Vietnam, Taiwan and Hong Kong; investment in, or expansion of, existing and new higher education facilities throughout Okinawa, including satellite campuses and collaborative scientific programmes; continued promotion of Okinawa as a high-profile international sports venue; and the designation of special fishing and environmental protection zones to conserve the island's unique marine environment while also sustaining its most iconic maritime industries.

Based on a common-sense understanding of Okinawan interests and the relevant available survey data, all of the above would almost certainly have the backing of a majority of the local population, as well as support from Okinawa's democratically elected political leaders across municipal assemblies. They in turn should be able to unite behind pressing their respective national representatives and LDP colleagues in Tokyo to make the relatively subtle changes required in order to realize a series of pertaining policy implementations. In this way it should, therein, be possible to effectively co-opt Okinawa's four sitting National Diet members. As noted earlier in the volume, at the time of writing two of these represent the government in LDP-held seats. However, Okinawan Diet representatives that are not standing as independents already have to strike a careful balance between their party line and being seen to promote Okinawan causes, so are vulnerable in that sense to popular pressure. In that regard, a coherent set of constructive policies that are realistic in their aims but avoid directly challenging either the progressive or conservative ideological factions, or the authority of central government, would seem to be a sound and credible political move. These also need to be skilfully designed and enacted so that localized changes might ultimately offer a greater degree of autonomy for the prefecture. If this takes the form of a comprehensive package of policies with private sector backing that deepen Okinawa's regional ties, it is also likely to reduce the risk of the islands becoming a flashpoint. This is because it would disincentivize the private–public industrial complexes of each of those states to aggravate counterproductively over an area of potential shared growth. Probably the biggest challenge that lies within this proposal, however, rests in the implementation of even small or piecemeal changes that threaten to reduce or disrupt the activities of powerful vested interests. As also discussed in Chapter 3, these are typically inextricably linked to, and deeply embedded within, how the day-to-day business of Okinawa's political economy is run through its three core industries: construction, bases and tourism.

CONSTRUCTION, BASES AND TOURISM: LIMITED RESOURCES AND CONSTRAINED ECONOMIC POTENTIAL

The preceding scenario, based on extended discussion throughout this volume, reinforces the argument that political decisions on Okinawa are, more often than not, driven primarily by economic interests. Indeed, this has been shown to be the case throughout the post-reversion era. Our exposition of concrete-based construction, the base economy and tourist industries further revealed the extent of this reality in these three key sectors. As such, these industrial-scale vested interests, which are manifest widely in well-established corporations headquartered in Japan's major mainland cities, amount to arguably the single biggest obstacle in preventing substantive socio-economic change on the Okinawan islands. Furthermore, these interests have their own political arms embedded within Japan's infamous "iron triangle", comprising the ruling LDP, bureaucracy and big business. With this understanding, analysts frequently point to the endemic dominance of such structural power as the primary reason behind the limited transformation of Okinawa's enormous potential throughout its contemporary history. This line of analysis assumes an ongoing scenario of curtailed business as usual, rather than progressive innovation leading to a flourishing broader-based local economy that can act as a fulcrum for the greater integration of regional East Asian economies. It also suggests that the continued promotion and primacy of these three sectors is inevitable or highly likely and that their continuation should be presumed to lead Okinawa into a position of greater precarity. In response, conversely, it is worth interrogating the extent to which these industries and the economic structures that support them are essential to ensuring sustainable growth, stability and prosperity across the prefecture.

If we assume that a higher degree of political self-determination coupled with increased economic independence of some kind are essential components of, or at least relevant contributing factors to, setting Okinawa on a course towards extended peace and prosperity, then these deeply entrenched mainland industries are a serious impediment. This is because they effectively monopolize markets, dominate Okinawa's limited physical space and create a significant degree of dependency for indigenous Okinawan enterprises upon actors on the Japanese mainland. As a range of empirical evidence exposed in the preceding chapters, the specifics of each case are somewhat distinct, but each key sector poses a comparable challenge in terms of their negative impacts in these regards. Moreover, their cumulative combined effect works to marginalize and limit radical reform of the prefectural political economy. This includes a complex confluence of entangled interests that require unpicking if they are to be effectively addressed. In that sense, it is useful to reflect on the nuances of each industry, in isolation, as separate but integrated variables that require further engagement.

Although often the most politically charged, the economic challenges posed by the so-called base economy are actually in some ways the least significant here, as their salience is diminishing with the restructuring and redeployment of US military assets. As the American forces' footprint decreases on the islands, so too should the already limited actual contribution of, and reliance on, bases as a source of local employment and consumer revenue. However, one of several serious concerns in this regard is the likelihood of JSDF stations replacing US facilities or supplementing those areas where there is a reduction in the stationing of US forces. Not only will this increase the probability of Okinawa becoming a double target – given the value to any adversary of damaging American *and* Japanese defence fixtures – it also means that many of the existing patterns of economic over-reliance or dependence observed in the Okinawan municipalities close to the bases will endure. These include low-paid and precarious employment, sprawling entertainment quarters and franchised hospitality chains that effectively keep Okinawans living in these areas locked in a cycle of limited social mobility, economic disadvantage and minimal opportunities to develop local industries and commercial enterprises. Furthermore, notorious examples such as the protracted relocation of the MCAS Futenma base demonstrate that when it is inconvenient for the US to relocate its forces off Okinawa, or to a less central location within it, the American military simply continues to deploy forces and use the bases as it has done since it seized the land at the end of the Battle of Okinawa.

This is the case even when that means flaunting its own national safety regulations, such as failing to ensure a suitable surrounding clearance zone around the base away from residential buildings and critical infrastructure.

Undoubtedly, the lack of useable space on Okinawa – which, as noted, covers only 0.6 per cent of the total Japanese land mass – is a serious limitation when it comes to infrastructural development; something that is made worse by over 20 per cent of that land being clogged up with military bases. One might think, then, that the construction industry would be essential in getting new infrastructure built as a means to partially alleviate some of the congestion caused by hosting expansive military facilities, such as Kadena Air Base and MCAS Futenma. This includes the provision of new roads and monorail lines, as well as a new runway for Naha International Airport and the massive reclamation of land around Okinawa's coasts already discussed. There are, indeed, huge levels of investment into these mega infrastructure projects. Correspondingly, they have a significant impact on the islands in terms of their stimulation of the local economy through improved access routes and attractive residential housing projects. However, the reality is that an unending series of construction sites, including the new base at Henoko, also continue to act as a means by which large private enterprises from outside of the prefecture siphon off public funds that are ostensibly allocated to benefit Okinawa more broadly. Instead, Okinawans mostly work on these projects in low-ranking, low-skilled and low-paid roles, whereas giant profits are gained by their mainland corporate bosses who are not held accountable for the extent to which they are actually benefiting living standards on Okinawa. Hence, without regulatory intervention at the political and bureaucratic levels, this trend is set to continue.

A similar pattern prevails in the tourist sector. Here, mainland companies also dominate through the ownership and running of hotel resorts, package tours, and theme parks or other one-stop attractions. Many such projects and facilities, as well as the noted creation of a second runway at Naha International Airport, are presented at the time of approval as inward investment into the prefecture. This is true in purely financial transactional terms, but these corporate exploits do not necessarily enrich many Okinawans. Rather, as with the case of the construction contractors that are effectively siphoning off public funds into the private sector, the domination of some of Okinawa's most valuable coastal sites is undertaken by large mainland enterprises. These are often supported by local government but typically only enrich a small number of wealthy business owners and, to a lesser or less obvious extent, local officials. In contrast, resorts and theme parks deny the use of these pristine stretches of real estate to a larger number of actors for a broader range of commercial, social and environmental endeavours. All of this reinforces the claim that Okinawa, as the once independent Ryukyu Kingdom, today remains in one sense a colony of Japan, and by extension the US–Japan alliance, rather than a truly equal prefecture within the appropriate body politic.

In light of these aspects, the surge of post-pandemic overseas tourists has limited financial benefits for most local residents, as noted for instance in the discussion of Miyakojima Island (see Chapter 3). What is more, it does little to enhance smoother regional relations through Japanese soft power, or *smart* power, whereby industries such as tourism can play a key role in increasing bilateral grassroots communications and broadening exchange. Compounding this phenomenon, the lack of diverse benefits beyond individual spending by tourists occurs partly as visitors from countries such as China and elsewhere on mainland Asia are perceived to reinforce negative stereotypes and remain isolated from most forms of meaningful exchange or integration with Okinawan islanders. In that regard, a reframing may be necessary whereby, for example, tour companies and related tourism sector actors adapt their business models so as to demonstrate more cultural awareness and sensitivity to the local environments they impact upon visitation. In this respect, too, if left unaddressed as a significant socio-economic issue, local resentment directed towards mainland China in particular may grow rather than decrease if the tourist industry continues to expand through its current business models and practices on Okinawa. This comes as a by-product of the asymmetrical tourism-related practices outlined above, where, once again, the employment and exchange opportunities for locals are limited and low paid. Concomitantly, their largely superficial interactions with short-term incomers, in particular those from the PRC, often serve to entrench an already endemic suspicion felt towards Asia's largest economy and its citizens.

DIVERSIFYING THE OKINAWAN ECONOMY: INNOVATION AND NEW INDUSTRIES

Fortunately, the negative economic scenario in which big business continues to control an exploitative relationship in general alignment, if not cahoots, with central government to the detriment of local residents and claim dominion over their lands, is avoidable. Even more encouraging is the evidence that a notable number of incremental steps are currently being taken towards restructuring Okinawa's local economy in a positive direction. To date, these have mostly been led by the Prefectural Government, but an increasing number of private enterprises (both local and external to the prefecture) and non-profit organizations are becoming involved across a broad-based market, including various private–public collaborations. The key point here is economic diversification. As highlighted through the examination of investment into science and technology projects within the prefecture, the hosting of international sports events and camps, as well as ecotourism sectors promising sustainable initiatives, are all areas where Okinawa's considerable natural assets can be maximized. They are also being driven overtly to reduce tensions around the ECS rim under a flagship Okinawa Prefectural Government-led initiative promoting regional peace and prosperity. This means deliberate and proactive engagement with enterprises and governmental organizations in partner states around the ECS, including mainland China.

Despite incurring the ire of hardline conservatives opposed to engagement with the regime in Beijing, such efforts offer a model for conflict mitigation through a political economy-led approach. This is driven by transactional liberal exchange and economic integration. The promotion of such an approach also puts into practice the kind of rhetoric about win–win, positive-sum relationships espoused by all the relevant national governments involved. Thereby, they performatively bring into being the shared values of a rules-based order that advances prosperity and mutual respect for sovereignty. The challenge remains, however, as to how these promising exchange and trade initiatives can either supplant or, perhaps more realistically, coexist with the core industries of bases, construction and tourism on Okinawa. Of particular concern is how to expand the percentage of land that can be reutilized or reappropriated for more locally beneficial commercial activities, as well as how to increase the number of higher-paid or prospectively mobile employment opportunities for Okinawa's citizens.

In the case of bases, this would seem to be relatively straightforward. As noted above, as economic (mostly military budget-related) and political pressures mean that US forces on Okinawa are rationalized and reduced, the amount of land required for deploying troops and hosting equipment should also decline. This frees up land for use by actors from other sectors. However, if this somewhat simplistic outcome is to be realized in a timely and efficient manner, at least three important factors need to be accounted for: reclaimed base land should not simply be handed over for reuse as equivalent JSDF facilities; the reuse of land needs to be expedited as rapidly as possible after its return to ensure the tangible positive effects are felt within a meaningful time frame that encourages prospective investors; land reusage requires independent regulation and oversight to make sure that usage is indeed in the best interests of those living on Okinawa's islands. Without these provisions, real estate returned from former US military bases may, conversely, become the focal point for other kinds of controversy, including over security concerns that might actually serve to fuel regional disputes or rivalries. In that respect, lessons must be learned from the glacial process of relocating MCAS Futenma in this regard. In other words, despite popular opposition, as demonstrated via the 2017 referendum that opposed the new facility at Henoko, resistance to its construction has undoubtedly delayed the return of the existing facilities at Futenma. Hence, in this ongoing case, as well as in prospective cases to come, a degree of pragmatism should be applied. This is not to suggest capitulation vis-à-vis the GoJ, but rather that it can be used as a means to wrest control over the limited land space on Okinawa as quickly as possible, even if that means compromising so as to avoid militant opposition to certain kinds of unpopular developments.

In the case of the construction industries that rely so heavily on public works projects for their profits, relevant employers can be kept onside by being at least partially tasked with the redevelopment of the returned base sites, although the bidding system for contracts may need to be in a revised or specialized format. As part of this, government-led provisions should be put in place to ensure that the process does not again result in the creation of mostly only low-paid, labour-intensive jobs for Okinawans. In addition, local municipalities and populations could be allowed to have a principle say in the selection and design of the projects themselves. Similarly, in cases where these land redevelopment activities link directly to the tourist industry, equivalent regulations might also be designed on a sector-by-sector basis. They might reasonably include, for instance, the incentivization of ecotourism, diversification of multiple sectors and promotion of local enterprise buy-in to boost Okinawan ownership rates. Concomitantly, the prefectural authorities should also be able to encourage further cooperation or collaboration with surrounding ECS rim states, which would increase market-driven competition, bolster inward investment and promote cordial international relations. At the same time, if successful, the implementation of such policies would, again, disincentivize localized aggravation, avert overfortification of the First Island Chain through further basing and potentially even serve to improve regional security by calming simmering transnational disputes that threaten to envelope Okinawa.

HOW MUCH SECURITY IS ENOUGH SECURITY? BEWARE OF BIPOLARITY

The liberal vision, as sketched above, of an optimally integrated regional economy in which Okinawa plays a central, somewhat semi-autonomous, role as a bastion of enduring peace and prosperity is certainly an attractive one. It is also an eminently possible scenario given the right kinds of political will and economic know-how. However, as unpacked throughout the in-depth discussion in Chapter 4, there are more challenges here than merely the structural economic imbalances and vested interests noted in the first two scenarios. In the broader geostrategic security arena, there are serious threats to Okinawa's mid- to longer-term outlook. In simple terms, Okinawa remains on course to become a flashpoint between not only the world's three largest economies but also its two greatest geomilitary powers. And, despite vocal opposition from within the islands and elsewhere, fortification of the Okinawan archipelago continues at an unprecedented pace. This includes both the physical increase of JSDF bases and assets, including the noted missiles designed to strike mainland China, and how island defence is now conceptualized and practised for by the soon to be seamlessly integrated US and Japanese militaries.[1]

The political advocacy for increasing military strength over the Southwest Island Chain looks, in this regard, set to continue and prepares Okinawa as the key point, or "keystone", of defence for the US–Japan alliance against Beijing. Correspondingly, this also makes the islands potentially the most likely site from which to launch a counter-strike or island recapture operation in the event of a full-scale military contingency over Taiwan. This places the Ryukyu's historically peaceful archipelago in a precarious position. That precarity is made all the more salient, as laid bare through the discussion of political structures detailed in Chapter 2, by the extremely limited local political power that Naha currently wields. Specifically, this is in terms of its inability to garner any meaningful opposition to policies of escalation at the level of national foreign policy-making.

Sino-Taiwanese-Japanese disagreement over the disputed Senkaku Islands further complicates this picture. Therein, escalation amid an unstable status quo would mean that this relatively small, uninhabited maritime space in the ECS could have potentially catastrophic consequences as a trigger for broader regional conflict. As with the political and economic aspects concerning Okinawa's framing as a likely flashpoint, the key here is the level of dynamism surrounding geopolitical issues that might affect the current situation around the islets. As it stands, there are repeated Coast Guard standoffs across and within the portion of the ECS that is within Japan's EEZ and surrounds the Senkakus. Inside of this concentrated maritime zone, escalation management is generally seen to be in the interests of all parties concerned. Furthermore, in line with this understanding, the official US position of deliberate ambiguity in relation to both Taiwan and the sovereignty of the Senkaku Islands has thus far helped to mitigate the risks of any move, probably from Beijing, to dramatically alter the status quo, as intruding

1 Commitment to such a trajectory has been confirmed repeatedly by both sides, as per US Department of Defense Major General Pat Ryder's 11 April 2024 assertion that the two countries would "further bolster defense and security cooperation to allow for greater coordination and integration".

security forces cannot be sure of the American reaction. However, in recent decades, as China's economic and military power has grown relative to that of both Japan and the US, the credibility of this ambiguous position taken by the Americans has become increasingly fragile as an effective deterrent. In that sense, a scenario where China unilaterally and fundamentally attempts to shift the dynamic in its favour grows increasingly likely and difficult to prevent.

In some respects, this is already taking place over the Senkaku Islands. For example, although both Beijing and Tokyo operationalize their respective – heavily armed – coastguards to manage the situation, China has not only designated an ADIZ and recommissioned naval ships to out-muscle their JCG counterparts, but suspected government-backed militias and other grey-zone actors now regularly penetrate deep into Japan's sovereign maritime territory surrounding the uninhabited islets. Furthermore, despite legislative changes on both sides of the ECS to enable the respective legal use of lethal force, in contrast to China, neither the JSDF nor American naval forces are legally well-empowered to rapidly intervene in this deteriorating situation. In any case, for the time being they remain unwilling to do so for fear of escalating a skirmish that could rapidly spiral out of control. Therefore, a flashpoint could still be reached once China's combined official and unofficial forces in the area reach a sufficient degree of tactical superiority, or at least confidence, to the point where, for example, they attempt some form of physical landing on the islands.

Such events might also act as a harbinger of things to come for Taiwan. That said, even less reassuring from an Okinawan perspective is the knowledge that security across the Taiwan Strait could also further deteriorate independently from that of the Senkaku Islands, because the impact of that contingency would probably be felt in the latter. In either case, Okinawa's (formally Ishigaki City's) administration of the Senkakus and proximity to Taiwan puts its outlying inhabited islands, such as Yonaguni, Ishigaki and Miyakojima in particular, in danger of sooner, or probably somewhat later, becoming the site of direct engagement between massive military forces. Indeed, with the global picture increasingly becoming one in which great power rivalry is divided along polarized lines that pit the US and Japan against China and Russia – both authoritarian regimes that appear willing to flex their regional military might when pushed – the prospects for ultimately avoiding an escalation to hot war, or at least the increasing intensification of a new cold war, seem bleak.

SECURITY THROUGH SHARED CONCEPTS AND REGIONAL INTEGRATION

Of greater encouragement than much of the contrasting evidence presented within this volume is that history teaches us how current negative trends in the international arena may change or be reversed. Moreover, even if they do not, their outcomes may not result in worst-case scenarios. In the case of Okinawa's continued fortification, there are those, as represented by the likes of Mayor Nakayama of Ishigaki Island and his LDP Diet member counterparts on Okinawa's main island, who believe that peace and stability are best achieved through a position of strength. This includes the establishment of robust defence capabilities in close coordination with the US. Furthermore, as highlighted by the examination of Chinese, Taiwanese and Korean national security doctrines, such a concept is very much in line with those projected by a majority of the East Asia region's states. Indeed, the alignment of these narratives becomes all the more apparent when it comes to the discussion of maintaining a peaceful – or at least relatively secure – ECS community. In other words, the build-up of military power does not necessarily by default have to indicate the escalation of international tensions. It can instead form the foundations of mutual deterrence, which serves to disincentivize hostile actions by any party for fear of serious reprisal, thereby establishing the basis for deeper trade and exchange relationships to flourish in the commercial sphere under a rules-based system.

There are also positive domestic political considerations to take into account that are outside of Okinawa's – and indeed Japan's – control. In the case of Taiwan, for instance, presidential elections that ended controversial nationalist Tsai Ing Wen's tenure in Taipei's presidential office, and somewhat undermine her like-minded successor, William Lai, because of his narrow margin of victory, may make rapid escalation of the tense situation either side of the Taiwan Strait less likely.

If such proves to be the case, it automatically reduces the likelihood of Okinawa's outlying islands being subsumed within a geostrategic blockade attempted by Beijing while attacking the main island of its claimed breakaway province. It should also be noted that although it is somewhat complex and in no way uniform as a configuration on this issue, mainland China's leadership has seemingly welcomed the recent friendly overtures of Okinawa. These include not only direct contact from the Prefectural Government in Naha but also initiatives to rejuvenate closer Okinawa–Taiwan relations. This may seem counter-intuitive, but essentially Taipei is regarded by the CCP as a Chinese city, so there is no inherent perceived conflict of interest.

A comparable approach may also unfold or be adopted by the CCP on and around the Senkaku Islands. Here, too, although the islands are disputed between China, Japan and Taiwan, Beijing's claims are ultimately based on the same principles as those put forward by Taipei. In that sense, as the underlying dynamics of structural power shift in China's favour, positive exchanges leading to tacit agreement between Japan and Taiwan might also allow the CCP to piggy-back on Taiwanese statements within negotiations to leverage greater recognition of the dispute's legitimacy from Tokyo, as opposed to Japan's current position of the Senkakus being unequivocal Japanese territory. This line of advancement might prove particularly effective if the two parties are also in a warming phase of cross-Taiwan Strait relations. Additionally, when viewed from the Okinawan perspective, if the Okinawa Prefectural Government continues to successfully push for peace through building a regional community, the GoJ might be persuaded to shift its position somewhat under the pretext of local popular support towards incorporating a less severe or absolute position on the Senkaku Islands. There is little evidence that any of these changes are afoot, or that they are likely to be brought about by the current administrations. Nevertheless, they could become unavoidable in the face of continued US decline or isolationism. Tokyo might, therein, perceive a need to stabilize and bolster Sino-Japanese relations as China rises to ascendency in East Asia.

HOPES AND FEARS: FINAL THOUGHTS

Okinawa's future is uncertain. What the discussion throughout this volume has made clear, however, is that Okinawans should fear the continuation of a series of negative trends that threaten to once again transform their historically troubled, but in many ways still idyllic, peacetime islands into a geopolitical flashpoint. As documented above, these include: long-standing, unresolved, local and subnational political divisions; endemic structural economic oppression orchestrated from the Japanese mainland that at times borders on neocolonialism; and an unfortunate position within the regional security architecture as the keystone that links vital maritime spaces between the western Pacific and ECS.

Having delved deeper into these dynamics, it is clear that Okinawa needs to act as pragmatically as possible as a single entity. This is particularly the case when it comes to exercising the maximum agency available that can be leveraged in socio-political, environmental, economic and geostrategic spheres. In other words, a meeting of minds and locally led strategies is required in order to make constructive changes in the key spheres of politics, economics and security. Independence, devolution and increased self-determination all currently appear to be unattainable – and, based on recent opinion polls in the case of the former two at least, perhaps even undesirable – goals. However, from both political and socio-economic standpoints, the prefecture's population would surely need to rally around a renewed all Okinawa cause, or something equivalent to it, if positive change is to be realized. The challenge, then, comes down partly to selecting what to focus on, as well as how to frame initiatives for change. A carefully selected range of core issues led by Okinawa Prefecture, in closer partnership and consultation with leading local businesses and experts, in this respect, might enable the prefecture's voice to be heard with greater interest, and thereby contribute more meaningfully to shaping the relevant national-level policy-making processes that affect them.

If the pace of change in technological, scientific and socio-cultural domains on the islands is anything to go by, there is considerable cause for hope and optimism here. Moreover, these are all sectors where inward investment and the deepening of multilateral relationships, mostly at the regional level, are the key to success. This would indicate that Okinawa has more than sufficient potential to realize a collective goal of becoming a diverse hub for a range of integrated commercial, societal and environmental initiatives and projects that benefit East Asia as a whole. This is already empirically demonstrable from the nascent developments now completed and underway in higher education, ecotourism, international sports activities and cultural exchange programmes that are covered in this volume.

In addition to this empirical evidence, there is also reason to be optimistic from a theoretical standpoint. As demonstrated by the reworking, synthesis and reapplication of leading IR theories to Okinawa's surrounding security dynamics, it becomes clear that pessimistic – *realpolitik* – outcomes of interstate conflict are neither inevitable nor necessarily the most likely. In fact, if IR realism is combined with liberal and constructivist strands of the discipline, we have all the elements required for a positive conceptual, as well as pragmatic, approach to policy-making. Furthermore, there need be little if any inherent conflict of interest in a regionally centred approach that benefits the prefecture of Okinawa writ large and contributes to Japan's broader national interests. What is more, none of this denies the current harsh reality of a competitive struggle for power in the international system. Rather, it points to the fact that, as a regional keystone, Okinawa can be conceptualized, instrumentalized and – if limited to a carefully calibrated extent – robustly fortified, as a shining example of combined peaceful socio-economic endeavour and credible geomilitary deterrence achieved through strength. Amid this, even in a volatile global environment of geopolitical turmoil and rivalry, Okinawa's historical authenticity as a locus for antimilitarism and cordial coexistence should help it to not only project the almost universally endorsed rhetoric of peace through rules and order, but also to make it a reality.

Glossary

ame to muchi – candy and whip (carrot and stick)

CCP – Chinese Communist Party

East China Sea (ECS) – body of water between the northern tip of Taiwan, mainland China and the Okinawan archipelago

First Island Chain – string of islands running from mainland Japan through the Amami and Ryukyu Islands, including Okinawa, through to the islands between Taiwan and the Philippines

Government of Japan (GoJ) – Japan's central ruling authority

IJA – Imperial Japanese Army

ikkatsu kōfukin – annual lump sum payment from central government to Okinawa Prefecture

IR – International Relations (as a set of established theories forming the academic discipline)

JCP – Japan Communist Party

-jima **(*shima*)** – suffix for island (sometimes included officially within the island's name, as in Miyakojima Island)

JSDF – Japan Self Defense Force

keystone of the Pacific – Okinawa as designated by US military leaders in the Pacific War on account of its particularly significant geostrategic position in the western Pacific Ocean

Liberal Democratic Party (LDP) – Japan's conservative ruling party, in government for almost the entire period since 1955

omoiyari yosan – sympathy budget, paid by Japan's central government to US forces stationed on Okinawa for their maintenance and upkeep

PLAN – People's Liberation Army Navy

prefecture – primary unit of local governance for major local authorities in Japan (equivalent to a province in other countries)

Ryukyu Kingdom – former (semi-)autonomous kingdom that governed the Okinawan islands as a tributary state of dynastic China until formal annexation by Japan in 1879

Second Island Chain – string of islands running from mainland Japan east of the First Island Chain through the Mariana Islands and Guam to Palau

Senkaku Islands – uninhabited, disputed islets located between Okinawa's Yaeyama (Ishigaki) cluster, Taiwan and mainland China (Diaoyu in mainland China; Tiaoyutai in Taiwan)

suteishi – throwaway stone (Okinawa), used to describe how Okinawa was sacrificed by the IJA to blunt the Allied invasion of mainland Japan

Typhoon of Steel – metaphor for the Allied assault during the Battle of Okinawa

Further reading

To really understand why Okinawa matters so much, I would urge all those who read this book to spend time there. It is a truly special place. The food, the people and the shimmering coral seascapes all make these islands worthy of the title "keystone of the Pacific", regardless of the geopolitical significance attached to this term and its subject. Nevertheless, even for many of those fortunate enough to reach Japan, Okinawa's distance from the mainland means that a good portion of those souls never reach the islands to make up their own mind about its past, present and prospective future. As such, the following guide to further reading offers a selection of academic and non-academic sources, including those in both English and Japanese, as a practical means by which to gain a relatively informed and holistic picture of the issues discussed in the preceding chapters. These have been divided into three sections for ease of access, with each section ordered by relevance and scope from a would-be newcomer to Okinawa's perspective, that is with the most generally useable and significant sources annotated first, through to those with the most specific or obscure focuses.

ACADEMIC SOURCES

As a newcomer to the academic study of Okinawa, although somewhat overtly left leaning in terms of much of its scholarly content, *The Asia-Pacific Journal: Japan Focus* has consistently provided a powerful critique of contemporary Okinawan affairs by acclaimed academics in the field. This includes from the purely political and economic, through to intersections with environmental activism, anthropology and beyond, as exemplified by Marius Palz's article, "Okinawan coral politics, Henoko Base construction and a Japanese political strategy of ignorance" (2021). From a more centrist perspective, *East Asia Forum* also takes on the role of introducing key contested issues on Okinawa. In addition, Conversation UK offers a small but highly accessible set of short online articles, including those by the current author on base-related issue, published by Mason in 2017 and 2021,[1] and Paul Christensen's 2015 piece on the 70th anniversary of the Battle of Okinawa.[2]

Mainstream area studies journals, such as the *Pacific Review*, *Asian Survey* and *Journal of Japanese Studies*, are further rich sources for scholarship on Okinawa's socio-political, economic and geostrategic issues. In addition there are several specific additional works of academic interest that analyse security issues surrounding the Ryukyu Islands. These include: Rajaram Panda's article, "Japan sets up military base in Ishigaki to deter China" (2023); Raul Peter Pedrozo's related discussion of residual sovereignty, "US recognition of Japanese sovereignty over the Senkaku Islands" (2021); and Olivia Tasevski's "Okinawa's vocal anti-US military base movement" (2022). Mayu Konishi's "Senkaku Island issue between China and Japan" (2011) also offers valuable insights into Okinawa's embroilment in the region's key territorial dispute. These sources can be further engaged with from a legal perspective through work produced by the Constitute Project,[3] as well as through leading academic think tanks, such as the Institute for Defence Studies and Analyses and the Brookings Institution.

In terms of Japanese-language academic sources, specifically on the issue of island fortification, Keiko Kurihara's "Nansei shotō de susumu jieitai haibi: Amami ōjima, miyakojima, ishigakijima ga sensō saizensen ni [Deployment of JSDF forces progresses throughout the Southwest

1 Mason, "Why a row over military bases on Okinawa spells trouble for US–Japan relations", The Conversation, 2017, https://theconversation.com/why-a-row-over-military-bases-on-okinawa-spells-trouble-for-us-japan-relations-72685 and Mason, "US–Japan relations: why two new leaders need a fresh approach to the alliance in the Asia-Pacific", The Conversation, 2021, https://theconversation.com/us-japan-relations-why-two-new-leaders-need-a-fresh-approach-to-the-alliance-in-the-asia-pacific-154302.

2 Christensen, "Battle of Okinawa's legacy lives on 70 years later as locals chafe against Japanese rule", The Conversation, 2015, https://theconversation.com/battle-of-okinawas-legacy-lives-on-70-years-later-as-locals-chafe-against-japanese-rule-us-arms-39357.

3 See http://Constituteproject.org.

Islands: Amami Ōjima, Miyakojima and Ishigakijima move towards becoming a wartime front line]" (2019) offers a particularly insightful critique. Correspondingly, Gendairiron, in combination with the Peace Studies Association of Japan (PSAJ), both provide valuable sources of regular academic contributions on the topic of Okinawa and its prospects for maintaining a lasting peace.

NON-ACADEMIC SOURCES

The non-academic literature on Okinawa varies wildly in terms of its authority and accuracy. As such, accessing Okinawa-related topics from a variety of credible perspectives is challenging but essential in order to gain real insights. For the discussion of international disputes, viewing original legal sources can be highly informative, such as those provided through the United Nations Convention on the Law of the Sea. Similarly, the Asia Maritime Transparency Initiative's "Force majeure: China's coastguard law in context" (2021) provides further relevant content in illustrating recently enacted legal changes pertaining to the Senkaku Islands dispute. The respective government ministries of Japan and China also offer in-depth documentation and discussion from opposing points of view. These include the Ministry of Foreign Affairs of the PRC's statement, "Set aside dispute and pursue joint development",[4] and MOFA's official 13 December 2022 press release on the "Senkaku Islands". Meanwhile, a Japan MOD 2017 white paper further discusses the usage of land reclaimed from US base sites on the islands in its editorial, "Susumu okinawa no tochi henkan to atochi riyō" [Advancements in the return of Okinawan land its usages]. Related opinion poll data can also be found via the Japanese Cabinet Office's official webpages, such as the 2021 "Naikakufu yoron chōsa: beigunkichi/jieitai" [Cabinet opinion poll: American military bases and the Self Defense Forces].[5]

Outside of official websites and white papers, there is a wide range of news media sources that attempt authoritative coverage of Okinawa.

4 See https://www.mfa.gov.cn/eng/zy/wjls/3604_665547/202405/t20240531_11367540.html.

5 See https://survey.gov-online.go.jp/h12/h13-okinawa/2-5.html.

A number of standout outlets and pieces are worthy of mention here. These include Jon Mitchel's 2021 article for *The Intercept*, "NCIS case files reveal undisclosed US military sex crimes in Okinawa" (2021);[6] Douglas Lummis's piece, "Futenma: 'The most dangerous base in the world'" (2018); and Mathias Cena's AFP-Jiji article, "'Inevitable': views on US bases shift on Okinawa" (2022). The account, "50 years on from reversion, Yonaguni Island a shadow of its former self" (Jiji Press 2022) also provides a valuable contribution to the discussion. For broader coverage in a regional context, the Asia News Network, *Nikkei Asia*, *The Economist*, DW, *Japan Times* and *Nippon Keizai Shimbun* are all useful reference sources and can be readily searched for Okinawa-related articles via their respective websites. Among national news outlets, *Asahi Shimbun* is arguably the most balanced and objective in its coverage. Exemplar pieces include Abe Shunsuke's "Top court rules against Okinawa governor's bid to block new base" (2021) and the *Asahi Digital* entry, "Nansei shifuto wa 'okinawa no mondai' de wa nai: atomawashi ni sareta kokumin hogo no giron" [The southwestern shift is not an "Okinawan problem": debating the protection of citizens who have been deprioritized] (2023). The above are in contrast with the *Yomiuri Shimbun* and *Sankei Shimbun*, which have strong conservative political leanings.

As per the academic outlets already recommended, there are also several other key sources outside of the academy that provide specific analysis of pertinent security issues on Okinawa, although the financial backing and political support of all of these should be carefully considered. *Defense News*, *The Strategist* and Military.com all fall into this category. In addition, for controversial topics, there are alternative (to the mainstream) pieces worth reading, such as the *Catchy* article, "Kebin mea nihon buchō " [Kevin Maher, US–Japan Bureau Chief comments that 'Okinawan's are famous swindlers'] (2011), which documents the complicating impact of American commentary on Japanese domestic politics and society, as well as more scenario-based analyses in the manner of Shigeru Handa's online discussion, "Taiwan yūji de dō naru okinawa – nihon: Nihon, beigun – jieitai no tenkai 'handa shigeru no me' no. 65" [What would happen to Okinawa and Japan in the case of a

6 See https://theintercept.com/2021/10/03/okinawa-sexual-crimes-us-military/.

contingency on Taiwan: the transformation of US forces and the JSDF in Japan ("Shigeru Handa's perspective" no. 65)] (2023).

In order to gain a more holistic perspective, these should be absorbed in combination with analysis of the underlying economic shifts affecting the islands, as provided in the Keizai Shimbun article, "Umaranu hondo to no kakusa: dēta de yomu okinawa fukki 50 nen" [The disparity gap that doesn't close: interpreting 50 years of Okinawan reversion through data] (2022), and discussed further in "Is it true US military bases benefit Okinawa's economy?" (Mainichi Shimbun 2022). Equally, it is worth incorporating the environmentalist standpoints, primarily through materials produced by societal activists, including the *Tokyo Review* article by James Fisher, "The dark side of Japan's Okinawa boom" (2017), as well as 2023 statements from the Ōruokinawa kaigi [All Okinawa group] and Greenpeace. Ito Joi's blog post, "Cement and Japanese politics" (2008), further buttresses this discussion.

ENGLISH- AND JAPANESE-LANGUAGE OUTLETS ON OKINAWAN POLITICS

Finally, particularly for those able to either read Japanese or readily use software to translate it, the below offers a short, annotated list of sources specifically dedicated to the politics of Okinawa. In terms of addressing the issue of the prefecture becoming a flashpoint, Okinawa Prefecture's 5 October 2022 "Okinawaken ga futenma hikōjo no henoko isetsu ni hantai suru riyū" [The reasons why Okinawa Prefecture opposes the relocation of Futenma Airbase to Henoko],[7] is a useful starting point. In addition, summaries of public debates, such as the "Okinawaken shusai shinpojiumu 'kōryū – taiwa de tsukuru ajia taiheiyō chiiki no heiwa to mirai'" [Okinawa Prefectural Government hosted symposium "creating a peaceful future for the Asia-Pacific region through exchange and dialogue"] are accessible via the Okinawa Prefectural Government's homepage[8] or popular streaming platforms. The site also provides access to Okinawa Prefecture's official polling data, including on topics such as

7 See https://www.pref.okinawa.jp/heiwakichi/futenma/1017409/1017413.html.

8 See https://www.pref.okinawa.jp/.

"Beigun kichi to okinawa keizai ni tsuite" [Regarding the Okinawan economy and American bases] and "Gaikokujin kankōkyaku manzoku chōsa" [Foreign tourists satisfaction survey]. Equally useful sources can be found at the Okinawa Prefectural Government Washington DC Office and include online headings such as "U.S. Military Base Issues in Okinawa" and "U.S. bases and Okinawa's economy: transition of base-related revenue".

If visiting Okinawa in person, the Okinawa Prefectural Peace Memorial Museum is a must-see, but it also has an extensive, readily accessible online presence (including in English) that documents the politics, strategy and impact of the Battle of Okinawa. Further to the above, other national news media outlets, such as the *Tokyo Shimbun*, can be useful for assessing more recent developments via interviews with key actors. These include the 24 February 2022 article, "Henoko kenmin tōhyō sannen susumu kichi kensetsu 'hodo yūsen no kōzō kawarazu' jūmin tōhyō shudō shita asato nagatsugu shi ni kiku" [Three years on after the prefectural referendum on Henoko "the structure of prioritizing the mainland remains unchanged": we ask Asato Nagatsugu who directed the citizens' referendum], as well as providing detail on contrasting opinions, as per the 11 May 2022 *Asahi Shimbun* piece, "Survey: 41% in Japan OK with Okinawa bearing U.S. base burden", and the 13 January 2023 article, "Okinawa still burdened by legacy as Japan's 'military colony'". In addition, these issues are regularly discussed further in public debate forums (both online and in person) hosted by the Yokosuka Council on Asia-Pacific Studies.

For coverage from within the prefecture, there are a number of minor (limited-circulation) off-island local newspapers that pick up interesting political angles on the Yaeyama and Sakishima island clusters in particular, but the *Okinawa Times* and the *Ryukyu Shimpo* provide the most extensive discussion from around the prefecture. They are both usually in opposition to the Japanese central government and US military. Illustrative editorials include the 29 September 2022 *Okinawa Times* editorial, "'Gokochi ii kankyō de hatarakeru', 'kōkyo kōtsūmō no jūjitsuwo': hatten ga mezamashii toyosaki eria no mirai, kigyōdaihyōra teigen zokuzoku" ["Be able to work in a great environment", "fully develop the public transport network": business leaders make a splurge of proposals for the future of the Toyosaki area amid flagship development] and the *Ryukyu Shimpo* pieces of 16 January 2023 and 9 May 2023, "Minseiiinbusoku: yuimāru wo shakai seido ni" [Social worker shortage: turning Okinawan yuimāru community spirit into a societal system] and "Anzen hoshō seron chōsa 'heiwa kokka' rosen no kenji wo" [Public survey on security calls for the strengthening of a path towards a "peace state"].

Other one-off publications that provide thought-provoking opinion with a degree of expertise include: Keishi Koja's 15 December 2022 article for *Stars and Stripes*, "Long-range missiles for Okinawa should come with local buy-in, experts say", in addition to Seth Robson and Hana Kusumoto's 28 October 2022 piece, "Air Force to replace F-15s on Okinawa with more advanced fighters on rotation"; Kainan Corporation's "Okinawa no gunyōchi no rekishi (zenhen)" [The history of American military facilities on Okinawa (Part 1)] (n.d.); PSAJ's 100 points of political debate, "100 no ronten: 5. sengo nichibei kankei no naka de okinawa wa nan datta no deshō ka" [100 points of debate: no.5, how was Okinawa manifest within postwar Japan–US relations?],[9] and the communist perspective put forward by *Akahata Shimbun*, as per its 24 December 2022 article, "Okinawa shinkōhi sara ni genshō: Ikkatsu kōfukin wa kako saiteigaku ni" [Okinawa's development funding is further slashed: lump sum payment set to become the lowest on record].

9 See https://www.psaj.org/100points5/.

References

Abbasi, R. 2020. "Evolving security dilemma between the US and China: implications for regional strategic stability on South Asia". *Pakistan Horizon* 73(1): 55–77.

Abe, S. 2021. "Top court rules against Okinawa governor's bid to block new base". *Asahi Shimbun*, 7 July.

Ahmed, M. 2022. "China Coast Guard: on a trajectory for peace or conflict?" Center for International Maritime Security, 16 February.

Akahata Shimbun 2022. "Okinawa shinkōhi sara ni genshō: Ikkatsu kōfukin wa kako saiteigaku ni" [Okinawa's development funding is further slashed: lump sum payment set to become the lowest on record]. *Akahata Shimbun*, 24 December.

Akamine, M. 2017. *The Ryūkyū Kingdom: Cornerstone of East Asia*. Honolulu: University of Hawaii Press.

Aldous, C. 2003. "Achieving reversion: protest and authority in Okinawa, 1952–70". *Modern Asian Studies* 37(2): 485–508.

Aldrich, D. 1999. "Localities that can say no? Autonomy and dependence in Japanese local government". *Asian Journal of Political Science* 7(1): 60–76.

Allison, G. 2019. "Is war between China and the US inevitable?" Ted Talk. https://www.youtube.com/watch?v=XewnyUJgyA4.

Asahi Shimbun 2021. "Tokyo preparing for protracted battle over Henoko project". *Asahi Shimbun*, 26 November.

Asahi Shimbun 2022. "Survey: 41% in Japan OK with Okinawa bearing U.S. base burden". *Asahi Shimbun*, 11 May. https://www.asahi.com/ajw/articles/14618216.

Asahi Shimbun 2023a. "Okinawa still burdened by legacy as Japan's 'military colony'". *Asahi Shimbun*, 13 January. https://www.asahi.com/ajw/articles/14812976.

Asahi Shimbun 2023b. "Chūgoku niranda jieitai no bōei kyotenka, kyūsokuni susumu okinawa" [A "southwestern shift" to stare down China: strengthening of the JSDF defence hub across Okinawa is advancing at breakneck speed]. *Asahi Shimbun*, 13 May.

Asahi Digital 2023. "Nansei shifuto wa 'okinawa no mondai' de wa nai: atomawashi ni sareta kokumin hogo no giron" [The shift of focus to the southwest is not an "Okinawan problem: debating the protection of citizens who have been deprioritised"]. *Asahi Digital*, 13 May. https://www.asahi.com/articles/ASR5F5S6XR5DUTIL043.html.

Asia Maritime Transparency Initiative 2021. "Force majeure: China's coastguard law in context". Asia Maritime Transparency Initiative, 30 March.

Aso, T. 2023. "Jimin Aso Taro fukusōsai 'taiwan yūji de nihon nimo senka: bōeiryoku kyōka hitsuyō'" [LDP Deputy Head Aso Taro says "strengthened defence capability necessary as Taiwan contingency would spread to Japan"]. NHK, 9 January.

Bartok, A. 2022. "Islands in 'grey zone': Sino-Japanese arms race for the Senkaku Islands". Jagiellonian Conference on Security in Asia, Africa and Europe in cooperation with the DEEP Programme of NATO (updated version), University of East Anglia Centre for Japanese Studies Seminar Series, 27 October.

Bazhenova, Z. & E. Goriacheva 2023. "Unresolved problems of Okinawa: towards the 50th anniversary of Okinawa Prefecture's reversion to Japan". *Japanese Studies* 2: 73–86.

Becker-Weinberg, V. 2020. "South Korea boundary disputes in the East China Sea and the Yellow Sea". *Asia-Pacific Journal of Ocean Law and Policy* 5(2): 303–29.

Blanchard, B. & R. Woo 2023. "Taiwan warns of China's 'repeated provocations'". Reuters, 7 March.

Blank, S. 2019. "China's military base in Tajikistan: what does it mean?" *The Central Asia-Caucasus Analyst* 18. https://www.cacianalyst.org/publications/analytical-articles/item/13569-chinas-military-base-in-tajikistan-what-does-it-mean?.html.

Blaxell, V. 2010. "Preparing Okinawa for reversion to Japan: the Okinawa International Ocean Exposition of 1975, the US military and the construction state". *Asia Pacific Journal: Japan Focus* 8(29): 2–10.

Brunnstrom, D. & T. Hunnicutt 2022. "Biden says U.S. forces would defend Taiwan in the event of a Chinese invasion". Reuters, 19 September.

Bureau of Foreign Trade of the Republic of China 2023. Trade Statistics (official statement).

Burke, M. & K. Koja 2022. "Long-range missiles for Okinawa should come with local buy-in, experts say". *Stars and Stripes*, 15 December.

Catchy 2011. "Kebin mea nihon buchō 'okinawa no hito wa yusuri no meijin to hatsugen'" [Kevin Maher, US Japan Bureau Chief comments that "Okinawan's are famous swindlers"]. *Catchy*, 7 March. https://www.qab.co.jp/news/2011030726360.html.

Cena, M. 2022. "'Inevitable': views on US bases shift on Okinawa". AFP-Jiji, 13 October.

CGTN 2022. "China urges win–win cooperation after US and allies launch initiative in Blue Pacific". CGTN, 27 June.

Chang, R. 2023. "From chips to beyond: Taiwan's need for economic diversification". Harvard University Kennedy School Growth Lab, 15 May.

Chen, C.-C. & K. Shimizu 2019. "International relations from the margins: the Westphalian meta-narratives and counter-narratives in Okinawa–Taiwan relations". *Cambridge Review of International Affairs* 32(4): 521–40.

Chiavacci, D. 2022. "Social inequality in Japan". In R. Pekkanen & S. Pekkanen (eds), *Oxford Handbook of Japanese Politics*, 451–70. Oxford: Oxford University Press.

Constitute Project 2018. "Japan's Constitution of 1946". Article 95, 27 July. https://www.constituteproject.org/constitution/Japan_1946.

Costa, A. 2017. *The China–Japan Conflict over the Senkaku/Diaoyu Islands: Useful Rivalry*. Abingdon: Routledge.

CRS Service Report 2021. "The Senkakus (Diaoyu/Diaoyutai) Dispute: U.S. Treaty Obligations". 1 March, Congressional Research Service.

Dasgupta, A. 2023. "The Okinawa factor in Japan–China relations". Manohar Parrikar Institute for Defence Studies and Analyses, 4 August.

Davis, D. 2023. "Demonizing China gets the U.S. nowhere". Nikkei Asia, 4 May.

Dudden, A. 2019. "Okinawa today: spotlight on Henoko". In J. Kingston (ed.), *Critical Issues in Contemporary Japan*, 172–82. Abingdon: Routledge.

DW 2022. "Japan: what's behind Okinawa's falling life expectancy?" DW, 6 December. https://www.dw.com/en/japan-whats-behind-okinawans-falling-life-expectancy/a-62088176.

The Economist 2023. "Taiwan's dominance of the chip industry makes it more important". *The Economist*, 6 March.

Egami, T. 1994. "Politics in Okinawa since the reversion of sovereignty". *Asian Survey* 34(9): 828–40.

Endo, N. 2023. "Japan's westernmost island Yonaguni and Taiwan dream of renewed bonds". Asia News Network, 16 February.

Enloe, C. 2014. *Bananas, Beaches and Bases: Making Feminist Sense of International Politics*. Berkeley: University of California Press.

Feifer, G. 2000. "The rape of Okinawa". *World Policy Journal* 17(3): 33–40.

Feifer, G. 2001. *The Battle of Okinawa: The Blood and the Bomb*. Lanham, MD: Rowman & Littlefield.

Figal, G. 2012. *Beachheads: War, Peace and Tourism in Postwar Okinawa*. Lanham, MD: Rowman & Littlefield.

Fisher, J. 2017. "The dark side of Japan's Okinawa boom". *Tokyo Review*, 9 August.

Foreign Relations Committee 2023. "Evaluating US–China policy in the era of strategic competition". https://www.foreign.senate.gov/hearings/evaluating-us-china-policy-in-the-era-of-strategic-competition.

Foulon, M. 2015. "Neoclassical realism: challengers and bridging identities". *International Studies Review* 17(4): 635–61.

Gould, J. 2023. "Japan to OK new US Marine littoral regiment on Okinawa". *Defense News* (Pentagon), 11 January.

Greenpeace 2016. "Civil society condemns court ruling on US' Okinawa military base as undemocratic". Greenpeace press release, 16 September.

Gross-Stein, J. 1991. "Reassurance in international conflict management". *Political Science Quarterly* 106(3): 431–51.

Hagstrom, A. 2022. "White House once again walks back Biden's promise to defend Taiwan, says there is no 'policy change'". Fox News, 20 September. https://www.foxnews.com/politics/white-house-once-again-walks-back-bidens-promise-defend-taiwan-says-no-policy-change.

Hagström, L. & K. Gustafsson 2015. "Japan and identity change: why it matters in international relations". *The Pacific Review* 28(1): 1–22.

Handa, S. 2023. "Taiwan yūji de dō naru okinawa – nihon: Nihon, beigun – jieitai no tenkai 'handa shigeru no me' no. 65" [What would happen to Okinawa and Japan in the case of a contingency on Taiwan: the transformation of US forces and the JSDF in Japan ("Shigeru Handa's perspective" no. 65)]. 27 September.

Hasebe, Y. (ed.) 2015. *Kenshō anpo hōan: doko ga kenpō ihan ka* [Examining the Security Bill: where does it violate the constitution?]. Tokyo: Yuhikaku.

Hashimoto, R. 2019. "Hankichi undo to jānarizumu: 1950 nendai no Okinawa mondai hōdō wo jirei to shite" [The anti-military-base movement and journalism: press reporting on Okinawa in the 1950s]. *Rikkyo Journal of Social Design Studies* 18: 45–53.

Hatakeyama, K. 2023. "The Japan–US alliance and the Senkaku Islands: a source of conflict or strategically important?" Machinaka Com Centre, 31 January.

Hauken, K. 2020. *What Do We Talk about When We Talk about Prestige? An Examination of Conceptions of National Prestige in Japanese Parliamentary Discourse*. PhD dissertation, University of Sheffield.

He, K. 2017. "Explaining United States–China relations: neoclassical realism and the nexus of threat–interest perceptions". *The Pacific Review* 30(2): 133–51.

Hirano, M. 2014. "The maritime dispute in Sino-Japanese relations: domestic dimensions". *Asian Perspective* 38(2): 263–84.

Hiroshima Media Centre 2015. "Okinawasen shūketsu 70 nen 'suteishi' to shitsuzukeru no ka" [70 years after the conclusion of the Battle of Okinawa will it continue to be the "throwaway stone"]. Hiroshima Media Centre editorial, June.

Hong, Y. 2020. "Kadena Airfield: from auxiliary airstrip to 'Keystone of the Pacific'". In Y. Hong (ed.), *Comfort Stations as Remembered by Okinawans in World War II*, 196–232. Amsterdam: Brill.

Honrada, G. 2023. "China drone incursions drop a gauntlet on Japan". *Asia Times*, 4 January.

Hook, G. 2015. "The American eagle in Okinawa: the politics of contested memory and the unfinished war". *Japan Forum* 27(3): 299–320.

Hook, G., R. Mason & P. O'Shea 2015. *Regional Risk and Security in Japan: Whither the Everyday*. Abingdon: Routledge.

Hook, G. *et al.* 2011. *Japan's International Relations: Politics, Economics and Security*. Abingdon: Routledge.

Hoshino, E. 2013. "Okinawa no beigun kichi mondai to ningen no anzenhoshō" [Okinawa's US military base issues and human security], *Seisaku kagaku: kokusai kankei ronshū* [Policy Science: International Relations Collection], 15, *betsusatsu* [excerpts].

Hoshino, E. *et al.* (eds) 2018. *Okinawa heiwaron no ajenda: ikari wo chikara ni suru shiza to hōhō* [An Agenda for Okinawan Peace Studies: Viewpoints and Methodologies for Transforming Anger into Power]. Kyoto: Horitsu Bunkasha.

Hosoya, Y. 2019. "FOIP 2.0: the evolution of Japan's free and open Indo-Pacific strategy". *Asia-Pacific Review* 26(1): 18–28.

Howell, T. 2000. "Foreclosing a Japanese Hong Kong: Okinawa, 1967–1972". *Asian Perspective* 24(4): 243–71.

Ikeda, T. 2003. "War damage reconstruction, city planning and US civil administration in Okinawa". In C. Hein, J. Diefendorf & Y. Ishida (eds), *Rebuilding Urban Japan after 1945*, 127–55. Basingstoke: Palgrave Macmillan.

Ikenberry, J. 2009. "Liberalism in a realist world". *International Studies* 46(1/2): 203–19.

Japan Forward 2023. "Governor Denny Tamaki's silence on Senkakus a betrayal of Okinawans". *Japan Forward*, 13 July.

Japan MOD 2017. "Susumu okinawa no tochi henkan to atochi riyō" [Advancements in the return of Okinawan land its usages (editorial)].

Japan MOD 2023. "China's activities in East China Sea, Pacific Ocean and Sea of Japan". Official statement of Japan Ministry of Defense, February.

Japan Times 2016. "Plan to build base off Nago in 1960s given OK by US top brass". *Japan Times*, 4 April.

Japan Times 2017. "Revolving door politics". Editorial, *Japan Times*, 25 January.

Jiji Press 2022. "50 years on from reversion, Yonaguni Island a shadow of its former self". Jiji Press, 19 May.

Jiji Press News 2022. "All Okinawa-, LDP-backed candidates run for Naha mayor". Jiji Press News, 16 October.

Joi, I. 2008. "Cement and Japanese politics". Blog, 27 September. https://joi.ito.com/weblog/2008/09/27/cement-and-japa.html.

Junkerman, J. (dir.) 2016a. "Okinawa: the afterburn". Documentary, Siglio Productions.

Junkerman, J. 2016b. "Base dependency and Okinawa's prospects: behind the myths". *The Asian-Pacific Journal* 14(22). https://apjjf.org/2016/22/junkerman.

Kainan Corporation n.d. "Okinawa no gunyōchi no rekishi (zenhen)" [The history of American military facilities on Okinawa]. Kainan Corporation. https://www.kainanco.jp/blog/1236/.

Karimata, N. 2003. "Okinawa kara beihei ni yoru reipu jiken wo kokuhaku suru" [From Okinawa: uncovering rape cases by American soldiers]. Kokuminrengōkai, July. https://www.kokuminrengo.net/old/2003/200307-usbase-krmt.htm.

Kawamura, N. 2014. "Senkakushotō ryōyūken mondai to nicchu kankei no kōzōteki henka ni kansuru kōsai" [The disputed territorial rights of the Senkaku Islands and reconsideration of structural changes in Sino-Japanese relations]. Nagoya University, *Journal of School of Foreign Studies* 46(February): 27–51.

Kelly, T. 2022. "Japan's Okinawa may be on the front lines again as it marks anniversary of U.S. handover". Reuters, 12 May.

Kerr, A. 2001. *Dogs and Demons: Tales from the Dark Side of Japan*. London: Macmillan.

Kikuchi, N. 2002. "Baishun kinshi no gensetsu to gunji senryō: Beigun senryō shoki okinawa kara" [American occupation and the discourse of prohibiting prostitution: from the early period of American occupied Okinawa]. *Sociology* 46(3): 91–107.

Kim, H. 1973. "The Sato government and the politics of Okinawa reversion". *Asian Survey* 13(11): 1021–35.

Kobayashi, S. 2013. "Japanese historical reconciliation should begin at home with Okinawa". *Asia Pacific Bulletin*, East-West Center No. 218: 1–2.

Koikari, M. 2015. *Cold War Encounters in US-Occupied Okinawa*. Cambridge: Cambridge University Press.

Koja, K. 2022. "Long-range missiles for Okinawa should come with local buy-in, experts say". *Stars and Stripes*, 15 December.

Konishi, M. 2011. "Senkaku Island issue between China and Japan". The Ice Cases, Mandala Projects, July. http://mandalaprojects.com/ice/ice-cases/senkaku.htm.

Kurihara, K. 2019. "Nansei shotō de susumu jieitai haibi: Amami ōjima, miyakojima, ishigakijima ga sensō saizensen ni" [Deployment of JSDF forces progresses throughout the Southwest Islands: Amami Ojima, Miyakojima and Ishigakijima move towards becoming a wartime frontline]. *Gendai no Riron* 19(May). https://gendainoriron.jp/vol.19/column/col01.php.

Kyodo News 2018. "Japan and China launch communication mechanism to prevent air and sea clashes". *Kyodo News*, 8 June.

Lau, S. 2022. "China's top 5 wolf warrior diplomats sinking their fangs into Europe". *Politico*, 11 August.

Lauridsen, L. 2014. "Governance and economic transformation in Taiwan: The role of politics". *Development Policy Review* 32(4): 427–48.

Lummis, D. 2018. "Futenma: 'The most dangerous base in the world'". *The Diplomat*, 30 March.

Madison, C. 2019. "Tracking public support for Japan's remilitarization policies: an examination of elitist and pluralist governance". *Asian Journal of Comparative Politics* 4(2): 123–40.

Maeshiro, T. 2021. "Kurappu ronbun to okinawa henkan kenkyū no tenkai: kenzai shuken, kenedi shinseisaku, 'kakunuki hondo nami' no kettei" [Clap theory and developments in the research of Okinawa's reversion: residual sovereignty, Kennedy's new policy and the decision for "in-line with the mainland without nukes"]. *Handai Hōgaku* 71(3/4): 389–416.

Mainichi Shimbun 2022. "Is it true US military bases benefit Okinawa's economy?" *Mainichi Shimbun*, 9 September.

Manicom, J. 2014. *Bridging Troubled Waters: China, Japan, and Maritime Order in the East China Sea*. Washington, DC: Georgetown University Press.

Manyin, M. 2016. "The Senkakus (Diaoyu/Diaoyutai) dispute: US treaty obligations". Congressional Research Service Report 42761.

Mason, R. 2016. "Nationalism in Okinawa: Futenma and the future of base politics". *International Review of Ryukyuan and Okinawan Studies* 5: 15–44.

Mason, R. 2019. "Okinawa narratives: delineating rhetoric, policy and agency". *Japanese Studies* 39(2): 191–212.

Mason, R. 2023. "Layered security on Okinawa: reconciling international, national, and subnational narratives". In K. Nakatsuji (ed.), *Japan's Security Policy*, 117–39. Abingdon: Routledge.

Mason, R. & S. Park 2024. "Simmering storm in the East China Sea: shifting dynamics in the great power rivalries of East Asia". *Journal of Asian*

Security and International Affairs 11(3). https://journals.sagepub.com/doi/10.1177/23477970241261424.

Matsuda, M. 1967. *The Government of the Kingdom of Ryukyu, 1609–1872*. PhD dissertation, University of Hawaii.

Matsumura W. 2015. *The Limits of Okinawa: Japanese Capitalism, Living Labor, and Theorisations of Community*. Durham, NC: Duke University Press. McCurry, J. 2011. "US sacks diplomat over remarks about Okinawans". *The Guardian*, 10 March. https://www.theguardian.com/world/2011/mar/10/us-sacks-diplomat-remarks-okinawans-japan.

McDevitt, M. *et al.* 2012. "The Long Littoral Project: East China and Yellow Seas – a maritime perspective on Indo-Pacific security". Center for Naval Analyses, September. https://www.cna.org/reports/2012/IOP-2012-U-002207-Final.pdf.

McLauchlan, A. 2014. "War crimes and crimes against humanity on Okinawa: guilt on both sides". *Journal of Military Ethics* 13(4): 363–80.

MFA PRC 2023. "Foreign Ministry Spokesperson Wang Wenbin's regular press conference on April 18, 2023". Ministry of Foreign Affairs of the People's Republic of China, 18 April.

Midford, P. 2024. "The confrontation over the Senkakus and the transformation of Japan's security strategy during the Abe and Suga administrations". *明治学院大学国際学研究= Meiji Gakuin Review International & Regional Studies* 64: 29–55.

Mitchel, J. 2022. "The Okinawa system: the US military and the 1970s' narcotics trade". *Okinawa Times*, 22 July.

Mitoma, T. 2014. "Futenma hikōjo mondai kara 'futan' to 'byōdō' wo kangaeru" [Considering "burden" and "equality" from the issues of Futenma airbase]. *Kyushu Kokusai Daigaku KyōyōKenkyū* 20(2): 20–41.

Miyauchi, H. 2016. "Formation and development of an Okinawan global network using an island hub". In M. Ishihara, E. Hoshino & Y. Fujita (eds), *Self-determinable Development of Small Islands*, 33–54. Singapore: Springer.

MOFA 2008. "Japan–China joint press statement: cooperation between Japan and China in the East China Sea". Ministry of Foreign Affairs of Japan, 18 June.

MOFA 2013. "Statement by the Minister for Foreign Affairs on the announcement on the 'East China Sea Air Defense Identification Zone' by the Ministry of National Defense of the People's Republic of China". Ministry of Foreign Affairs of Japan, 24 November.

MOFA 2022. "Senkaku shotō (Senkaku Islands)". Ministry of Foreign Affairs of Japan.

MOFA 2023. "China's activities in East China Sea, Pacific Ocean, and Sea of Japan". Ministry of Foreign Affairs of Japan, February.

Mukai, Y. 2023. "Taiwan contingency war game highlights Japan's critical importance". *Yomiuri Shimbun*, 22 April.

Nagamine, A. 2022. "Japanese innovation and the Okinawa Institute of Science and Technology". Yokosuka Council on Asia Pacific Studies, 26 September.

Nagayama, K. 2023. *Okinawa Tamashii*. Tokyo: Naigai Shuppan.

Nagy, S. 2022. "Okinawa's elections expose problems with military co-existence". *East Asia Forum* 5, October. https://eastasiaforum.org/2022/10/05/okinawas-elections-expose-problems-with-military-coexistence/.

Nakamura, R. 2021. "US to build anti-China missile network along First Island chain". *Nikkei Asia*, 5 March. https://asia.nikkei.com/Politics/International-relations/Indo-Pacific/US-to-build-anti-China-missile-network-along-first-island-chain.

Nakatsuji, K. 2023a. "How did Japan take the Taiwan Strait Crisis of 1995–6?" In K. Nakatsuji (ed.), *Japan's Security Policy*, 140–54. Abingdon: Routledge.

Nakatsuji, K. 2023b. "Has Japan finally become a reliable partner?" Yokosuka Council on Asia Pacific Studies talk at Misawa International Centre, 23 January.

Nakazawa, K. 2023. "Why China rolled out the red carpet for Okinawa governor". *Nikkei Asia*, 13 July. https://asia.nikkei.com/Editor-s-Picks/China-up-close/Analysis-Why-China-rolled-out-the-red-carpet-for-Okinawa-governor.

Nakazawa, T. 2021. "Ekotsūrizumu ni okeru chiiki zukuri ni muketa jūmin no shutai keisei: Okinawaken higashison wo jirei ni" [Citizens structural formation geared towards locality building through ecotourism: Okinawa's Higashi Village as a case study]. *Kankyō Kyōiku* 31(1): 13–22.

Namihira, T. 2014. *Kindai higashiajiashi no naka no ryūkyū heigō: chūka sekai 99chitsujo kara shokuminchi teikoku nihon e* [Ryūkyū Annexation amid Modern East Asia: From the Chinese World Order to the Japanese Colonial Empire]. Tokyo: Iwanami Shoten.

Nguyen, D. 2012. *Tourism Development in Okinawa: Spatial and Temporal Patterns*. MA thesis, Department of Geography and Environment, University of Hawaii.

Nihon Keizai Shimbun 2022. "Umaranu hondo to no kakusa: dēta de yomu okinawa fukki 50 nen" [The disparity gap that doesn't close: interpreting 50 years of Okinawan reversion through data]. *Nihon Keizai Shimbun*, 13 May.

Nippon Keizai Shimbun 2023. "Okinawaken no tamaki denii chiji, chūgoku hōmon ni 'tashikana tegotae'" [Okinawan Prefectural Governor Tamaki Denny, claims a "positive response" from his visit to China]. *Nippon Keizai Shimbun*, 7 July.

Nishiyama, H. 2022. "Base built in the middle of 'rice fields': a politics of ignorance in Okinawa". *Geopolitics* 27(2): 546–65.

O'Hanlon, M. 2022. "Getting China right: resoluteness without overreaction". Brookings Institution, 2 August.

OIST 2018. "Coral farming to help restore dying reefs". Press release, Okinawa Institute of Science and Technology, 17 May.

Okinawa Peace Memorial Museum 2022. "The basic concept of the Okinawa Prefectural Peace Memorial Museum". http://www.peace-museum.okinawa.jp/english/index.html.

Okinawa Prefectural Government 2012. "Basic plan for 21st century vision of Okinawa". Okinawa Prefectural Government, 13 March.

Okinawa Prefecture Government 2016. "U.S. bases and Okinawa's economy: transition of base-related revenue". Okinawa Prefectural Government, Washington, DC office.

Okinawa Prefectural Government 2021. "Hondo fukki 50 nen ni muketa zaioki beigun kichi no seiri – shukushō ni tsuite (yōsei)" [(request) Concerning the organization and reduction of US military bases on Okinawa 50 years after reversion to mainland Japan]. Okinawa Prefectural Government, May.

Okinawa Prefectural Government 2022. "Heiwa de yutakana okinawa no jitsugen ni muketa arata na kengisho" [A new proposal for the realisation of a peaceful and prosperous Okinawa]. Official pamphlet, Okinawa Prefectural Government, May.

Okinawa Prefectural Government 2023. "Kōryū – taiwa de tsukuru ajia taiheiyō chiiki heiwa to mirai" [Future regional peace in the Asia-Pacific constructed through exchange and dialogue]. Panel discussion event, Naha, 14 March.

Okinawa Times 2015. "'Okinawa crying out': history of protecting prefecture residents livelihood originates in 'island-wide land struggle'". *Okinawa Times*, 26 May.

Okinawa Times 2022a. "'Omoiyari yosan gōi': mienai Okinawa no futan" ["Sympathy budget agreement": no sign of a reduced burden for Okinawa]. *Okinawa Times*, 23 December.

Okinawa Times 2022b. "'Gokochi ii kankyō de hatarakeru', 'kōkyo kōtsūmō no jūjitsuwo': hatten ga mezamashii toyosaki eria no mirai, kigyōdaihyōra teigen zokuzoku" ["Be able to work in a great environment", "fully develop the public transport network": business leaders make a splurge of proposals for the future of the Toyosaki area amid flagship development]. *Okinawa Times*, 29 September.

Okinawa Times 2023a. "Ishigaki ni rikuji chūtonchi kaisetsu" [GJSDF base opens on Ishigaki]. *Okinawa Times*, 16 March.

Okinawa Times 2023b. "Higunji de chūgoku ni taiō" [Respond to China in non-military form]. *Okinawa Times*, 21 March.

Okinawa Times 2023c. "Shūkinpei shi, okinawa no rekishi ni genkyū 'jinmin nippō' de ryūkyūkan ya kumesanjūrokusei: tamaki denii chiji no hōchū wo ishiki ka" ["People's Daily" discusses the Ryukyu family and Kumei Rokusei migrants, as it reports that Xi Jinping made comments about Okinawan history: does this suggest cognizance of Governor Tamaki Denny's visit to China?]. *Okinawa Times*, 9 June.

Okubo, J. 2009. *Maboroshi no shima okinawa* [Okinawa: Island of Illusions]. Tokyo: Tankobun.

Okubo, J. 2015. *Okinawa no futsugō no shinjitsu* [The Uncomfortable Truth of Okinawa]. Tokyo: Tankobun.

Ouchi T. 2002. *Mitsuboekijima: waga saisei no kaiso* [The Island of Secret Trade: Recalling Our Revival]. Naha: Okinawa taimususha.

O'Shea, P. 2015. "The East China Sea maritime and territorial dispute: a stand-off that suits everybody?" *Global Affairs* 1(4/5): 455–63.

O'Shea, P. 2019. "Strategic narratives and US military bases in Japan: how 'deterrence' makes the Marine base on Okinawa 'indispensable'". *Media, War & Conflict* 12(4): 450–67.

Palz, M. 2021. "Okinawan coral politics, Henoko base construction and a Japanese political strategy of ignorance". *Asia Pacific Journal: Japan Focus*, 15 December.

Pan, Z. 2007. "Sino-Japanese dispute over the Diaoyu/Senkaku Islands: the pending controversy from the Chinese perspective". *Journal of Chinese Political Science* 12: 71–92.

Panda, R. 2023. "Japan sets up military base in Ishigaki to deter China". Vivekananda International Foundation, 24 March.

Patalano, A. 2014. "Seapower and Sino-Japanese relations in the East China Sea". *Asian Affairs* 45(1): 34–54.

Pedrozo, R. 2021. "US recognition of Japanese sovereignty over the Senkaku Islands". *International Law Studies* 97(1). https://www.spf.org/islandstudies/research/a00028.html.

Pilger, J. 2017. *The Coming War with China: A Film by John Pilger*. ITV, Dartmouth Films.

Rabson, S. 2012. "Henoko and the US military: a history of dependence and resistance". *Asia-Pacific Journal* 10(4). https://apjjf.org/2012/10/4/steve-rabson/3680/article.

RAND 2020. "An interactive look at the U.S.–China military scorecard". RAND Corporation. https://www.rand.org/paf/projects/us-china-scorecard.html.

Reed-Fouts, M. 2021. *Addressing the Status of Forces Agreement in Okinawa, Japan*. MA thesis, Department of International Studies, University of Oregon.

Reuters 2010. "Tokyo urges Japan, China to avoid tit-for-tat claims". Reuters, 21 October.

Rittenhouse-Green, B. & C. Talmadge 2022. "Then what? Assessing the military implications of Chinese control of Taiwan". *International Security* 47(1): 7–45.

Robinson, E. 2015. *Lost in Translation: US Forces and Crime in Japan*. MA thesis, Naval Postgraduate School, University of Maryland.

Robson, S. & H. Kusumoto 2022. "Air Force to replace F-15s on Okinawa with more advanced fighters on rotation". *Stars and Stripes*, 28 October.

Ryall, J. 2020. "Japan takes the high ground over its outlying islands". DW, 29 May. https://www.dw.com/en/japan-takes-the-high-ground-over-its-outlying-islands/a-53617175.

Ryukyu Asahi 2023. "'Okinawa to jieitai': Hangeki nōryoku wo yū suru misairu no kennai haibi" ["Okinawa and the JSDF": deployment of counter-strike capability missiles within Okinawa Prefecture]. Ryukyu Asahi Hōsō debate, 28 February.

Ryukyu-history.com 2017. "Ryukyu ōkoku ga shite ita chōkō bōeki ni tsuite" [Concerning Chinese tributary trade conducted by the Ruyukyu Kingdom]. Ryūkyū ōkoku – Okinawa no rekishi [Ryukyu Kingdom: History of Okinawa], 29 March. https://www.ryukyu-history.com/ryukyu-history/post-123.

Ryukyu Shimpo 2014. "Monkashō ga taketomichō kyōi ni zenkoku hatsu no zesei yōkyū: yaeyama kyōkasho" [National first as MEXT demands Taketomi Town Board of Education makes correction: Yaeyama textbook case]. *Ryukyu Shimpo*, 15 March.

Ryukyu Shimpo 2018. "Ishigaki mayor agrees to receive Japan Ground Self-Defense Force troops". *Ryukyu Shimpo*, 18 July.

Ryukyu Shimpo 2023a. "Minseiiinbusoku: yuimāru wo shakai seido ni" [Social worker shortage: turning Okinawan yuimāru community spirit into a societal system]. *Ryukyu Shimpo*, 16 January.

Ryukyu Shimpo 2023b. "Anzen hoshō seron chōsa 'heiwa kokka' rosen no kenji wo" [Public survey on security calls for the strengthening of a path towards a "peace state"]. *Ryukyu Shimpo*, 9 May.

Sakurazawa M. 2014. "Okinawa fukki zengo no keizai kōzō" [The structure of Okinawa's economy before and after reversion]. *Shakai Kagaku* 44(3): 33–46.

Sakurazawa, M. 2016. "Okinawa gendaishi no naka no shimagurumi tōsō no keifu" [Lineage of Okinawan contemporary history's island-wide protests]. *Rekishigaku Kenkyu* 949(October): 20–29.

Sato, K. 2019. "The Senkaku Islands dispute: four reasons of the Chinese offensive – a Japanese view". *Journal of Contemporary East Asia Studies* 8(1): 50–82.

Sato, Y. & A. Chadha 2022. "Understanding the Senkaku/Diaoyu Islands dispute: diplomatic, legal and strategic contexts". In M. De Souza, G. Coutaz & D. Karalekas (eds), *Asian Territorial and Maritime Disputes: A Critical Introduction*, 48–64. E-International Relations Publishing. https://www.e-ir.info/2022/06/23/understanding-the-senkaku-diaoyu-islands-dispute-diplomatic-legal-and-strategic-contexts/.

Schuman, M. 2023. "China could soon be the dominant power in Asia". *The Atlantic*, May.

Selden, M. 1971. "Okinawa and American colonialism". *Bulletin of Concerned Asian Scholars* 3(1): 50–63.

Shaw, H.-Y. 1999. "The Diaoyutai/Senkaku Islands dispute: its history and an analysis of the ownership claims of the PRC, ROC, and Japan". Occasional Papers No. 3, School of Law, University of Maryland.

Shimada, S. 2018. "Current situation and problems of the employment environment in Okinawa Prefecture". *Regional Studies* 22: 39–61.

Siddle, R. 1998. "Colonialism and identity in Okinawa before 1945". *Japanese Studies* 18(2): 117–33.

Son, K.-Y. and R. Mason 2013. "Building a maritime 'great wall' to contain China? Explaining Japan's recalibration of risk with the militarization of Okinawa". *Asian Perspective* 37: 437–61.

Stockwin, A. 1962. "Positive neutrality: the foreign policy of the Japanese Socialist Party". *Asian Survey* 2(9): 33–41.

Sumida, C. & T. Tritten 2011. "Ready or not, Okinawa aims to wean itself off of military dollars". *Stars and Stripes*, 20 August.

Takahashi, S. 2018. "Development of grey-zone deterrence: concept building and lessons from Japan's experience". *Pacific Review* 31(6): 787–810.

Takenaka, H. 2014. *Failed Democratization in Prewar Japan: Breakdown of a Hybrid Regime*. Stanford, CA: Stanford University Press.

Takizawa, M. 1971. "Okinawa: reversion to Japan and future prospects". *Asian Survey* 11(5): 496–505.

Tan, C. 2023. "China warns US about crossing 'red line' on Taiwan independence". *Nikkei Asia*, 7 March. https://asia.nikkei.com/Politics/China-People-s-Congress/China-warns-U.S.-about-crossing-red-line-on-Taiwan-independence.

Tanji, M. 2006. *Myth, Protest and Struggle in Okinawa*. Abingdon: Routledge.

Tanji, M. 2008. "US court rules in the 'Okinawa Dugong' case: implications for US military bases overseas". *Critical Asian Studies* 40(3): 475–87.

Tanji, M. & D. Broudy 2017. *Okinawa under Occupation: McDonaldization and Resistance to Neoliberal Propaganda*. London: Palgrave Macmillan.

Tasevski, O. 2022. "Okinawa's vocal anti-US military base movement". *The Interpreter*, Lowy Institute, 17 February.

Tokyo Shimbun 2022. "Henoko kenmin tōhyō sannen susumu kichi kensetsu 'hodo yūsen no kōzō kawarazu' jūmin tōhyō shudō shita asato nagatsugu shi ni kiku" [Three years on after the prefectural referendum on Henoko "the structure of prioritizing the mainland remains unchanged": we ask Asato Nagatsugu who directed the citizens' referendum]. *Tokyo Shimbun*, 24 February.

Trading Economics 2023. "China exports by country". https://tradingeconomics.com/china/exports-by-country.

Urashima, E. 2009. "Opting for the 'irrational': Tokyo brushes aside Okinawan court order to end Awase Wetlands Reclamation Project". *Asian-Pacific Journal: Japan Focus* 7(4). https://apjjf.org/urashima-etsuko/3025/article.

Uren, D. 2020. "Southeast Asia will take a major economic hit if shipping is blocked in the South China Sea". *Strategist*, 8 December.

Wang, V. & G. Stamper 2014. "Taiwan's policy toward the Diaoyu/Senkaku Islands dispute and the implications for the US". *Education About Asia* 19(2).

Watanabe, O. 2012. "Futatsu no kokuminteki keiken to shinjiyūshugi wo meguru taikō no shindankai: shinjiyūshugi seiji tenkan no kōsō to shutaikeisei ni shōten wo atete" [Two forms of citizens' experience and the new stage of opposing neoliberalism: focusing on the concepts and formulations of neoliberalism's political transformation]. *Rekishigaku kenkyū* [Journal of Historical Studies] 898(October): 2–12.

Watanabe, O. & T. Ono 2023. "Senkaku keibi no kaiho toppu ga kataru saizensen no riaru hikiwake kiipu jūyō" [The reality of frontline security of the Senkakus as told by the coastguard chief: "the importance of keeping things even"]. *Asahi Digital*, 29 March. https://www.asahi.com/articles/ASR3X72L7R3WTPOB002.html.

Williams, B. 2013. "The YIMBY phenomenon in Henoko, Okinawa: compensation politics and grassroots democracy in a base community". *Asian Survey* 53(5): 958–78.

Yan, X. 2006. "The rise of China and its power status". *Chinese Journal of International Politics* 1(1): 5–33.

Yellow Glasses 2019. "Okinawa yakuzashi" [Okinawan mafia history]. *Yellow Glasses*, 23 September. https://yellowglasses.jp/yakuza/.

Zhou, Y. 2021. "Vaccine nationalism: contested relationships between COVID-19 and globalization". *Globalizations* 19(3): 450–65.

Index